BASKETBALL

SKILLS, DRILLS AND SESSION PLANS

BASKETBALL

SKILLS, DRILLS AND SESSION PLANS

Alexandru Radu & Florin Nini

THE CROWOOD PRESS

First published in 2022 by
The Crowood Press Ltd
Ramsbury, Marlborough
Wiltshire SN8 2HR

enquiries@crowood.com
www.crowood.com

British Library Cataloguing-in-Publication Data
A catalogue record for this book is available from the British Library.

ISBN 978 0 7198 4145 3

Cover design by Sergey Tsvetkov

Acknowledgements
We would like to acknowledge the contribution of the following people and would like to express our deepest gratitude for their important contribution to this project: Keith Hunt, Mihai Tomescu and Adi Zaharia who provided us with wonderful photographs to illustrate the various points we made in the book; Alexandru Constantin Radu who drew beautiful diagrams that will help coaches understand the drills and exercises we proposed.

And finally, we would like to express our thanks and send love once again to our families (our wives and children) who supported us throughout the duration of the entire project and to whom we dedicate this book.
The Authors

Typeset by Simon and Sons
Printed and bound in India by Parksons Graphics

CONTENTS

INTRODUCTION

The rationale for this title comes from the authors' intention to produce an instrument that will help any basketball enthusiasts to get better and progress in order to improve the overall performance of the players and the teams they work with. Our main intention as coaches and as educators is to offer a book that contains high-level drills, exercises and session plans that will allow learning and continuous improvement to take place. The book is designed primarily as a resource for coaches and athletes (easy to use/easy to understand and apply in practice), but other readers such as Physical Education teachers, sport students who consider basketball coaching as an option for their future, volunteers or university lecturers who deliver basketball as part of their modules with undergraduate and post-graduate students will also find something useful in this book. Apart from the detailed description of the drill(s), the provision of the diagrams for each drill and additional photos will enhance the overall learning process.

After an introductory chapter that discusses the importance of drills as part of the training process and what to consider when selecting a particular drill, the book is divided into several chapters that are grouped around the main themes of drills for the various playing positions (individual drills for players who are playing the guard, forward and centre positions) and also drills for specific actions that are part of the game (offence and defence). The last two subchapters will be further subdivided into drills for individual defence and for team defence (and the same for offence), covering all that a coach will need to know when preparing their team for competition.

The book is constructed so that it achieves the following objectives:

- To offer expert advice on *what* to use and *how* to implement as part of the training process.
- To offer and to present clear drills and exercises that can be easily implemented into everyday coaching, with an indication of appropriate ways to progress and modify the drill in order to make it harder or easier; coaching points relevant to each drill have also been included.
- To provide a useful reference tool for basketball coaches and educators who are active at various levels of the game.

Most of the drills are currently in use as part of the training programmes delivered by the two authors after years of experience of working with various teams and players – it is worth mentioning that both authors coached at all levels of the game, including national team level, juniors and seniors, beginners, advanced and elite (professional) level in both the men's and women's game.

The basketball journey is exciting and rewarding – we hope you enjoy it!

KEY TO DIAGRAMS

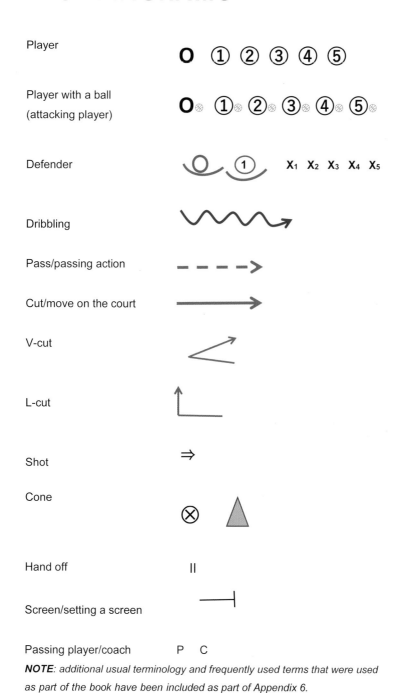

Player

O ① ② ③ ④ ⑤

Player with a ball
(attacking player)

O ① ② ③ ④ ⑤

Defender

X₁ X₂ X₃ X₄ X₅

Dribbling

Pass/passing action

Cut/move on the court

V-cut

L-cut

Shot

Cone

Hand off

Screen/setting a screen

Passing player/coach   P   C

NOTE: *additional usual terminology and frequently used terms that were used*
as part of the book have been included as part of Appendix 6.

DRILLS AS PART OF THE COACHING PROCESS – CONSIDERATIONS FOR COACHES

'Practice makes perfect' is an old saying – and this is perfectly applicable to the game of basketball. Repetition and the tens and hundreds of hours of hard work will allow individuals to master the fundamental elements and skills of the game. Knowing what to practise, when, for how long and with what intensity are vital components of the basketball coaching process; and this is what the book will try to achieve – to help you, the basketball enthusiast, to get better at playing and coaching the game at an individual level and at a collective (team) level too.

IMPORTANCE OF DRILLS

One of the main responsibilities a coach has is to conduct practices. Using drills when coaching is the most popular method of training players and teams. The main advantage of using drills is that it allows the coach to incorporate them during any part of the training session (during the warm up, main part and even in the warm down). In order to maximize their effect and impact on players (and on teams), drills can be used in isolation but also in combination with other activities such as exercises, small-sided games, relays and various competitive activities.

Lots of basketball coaches love the idea of running drills. But what are these drills? 'Drill' is a generic name given to certain activities that are designed to learn, to practise, to improve and/or to further develop a particular game-related component or more, for example a technical element such as passing, dribbling or a combination of two or more elements such as passing and shooting. By using drills as part of the training process you as a coach will improve your players and the team(s) you are working with, your practices and even improve your skills as a coach and those of any other assistant coaches you work with. As general advice, it would be useful to create for yourself different folders (even video folders) for different drills – for example drills for defence, drills for dribbling, drills for shooting, and so on, similar to how this book is structured.

WHAT TO CONSIDER WHEN SELECTING A DRILL

Is there a 'right way' when teaching a drill or when introducing a new aspect that you as a coach want your players to learn, for example a new skill, maybe a new drill, a new exercise? It is very likely that the answer is 'no' – there are no strict rules in this type of situation. But there are certainly solutions and considerations that are more suitable than others, depending on the context in which you as a coach operate. It all starts with the introduction of what you want to teach. This introduction must cover all the most important aspects of the drill but in a way that will not overwhelm the participants with too much information.

For any coach, there are a few considerations to be taken into account when it comes to planning and selecting the content of the training session. Some of the ideas presented below will help coaches to be effective in their choice/selection of drills:

- Have a clear aim and know exactly what you are trying to achieve in each session, even in each component part of the session.
- Make the drills *competitive* whenever possible. In this way the competitive element that all players enjoy will be present in the session and the competition will reduce the repetitive nature of some of the drills. Alongside this, the *fun* element does not need to be forgotten – this is what players of all ages like!
- Make sure you are aware of the *space* available when coaching and also the *equipment* you have access to (such as the number of baskets/hoops, basketballs, bibs or cones) so that you adapt the drill to the environment you operate within.
- It is important to know the *ability* of your players and their age – some drills could be adapted so that they could be used by beginners and/or younger

players; similarly, drills can be made more challenging when working with more advanced players – in this way you get the player(s) to work and achieve the aim you have planned for, such as to learn passing with two hands or to practise defensive slides. On a similar point, it is equally important to remember to include all the players and then conduct the drill so that it eliminates (or at least reduces) the players' waiting time at the back of the queue.

- Consider the principle of *progression* when using a new drill – start with an easy drill then add various levels of difficulty and complexity.
- *Variability* – using the same drill over and over again will mean players (beginners especially) become bored very quickly! Cross and Lyle presented this idea, saying: 'Repetitive work eventually becomes boring, and that applies to beginners as much as it does to elite athletes!' (Cross and Lyle, 2002, p. 77). As coaches we all have our preferences and it is down to you as an individual to have a set of perhaps four or five drills that you can adapt and modify according to your needs (and these needs could be, for example, number of participants, length of the training session or moment of time during the season).
- The *time* available for the session as well as the preparation stage (the moment in time during the season) for the players and team need to be taken into account, for example certain drills could be used during the pre-season stage, in-season or post-season). In addition to this, the time spent on training, on competitions and on any other amount of physical activities that the player(s) will undertake at school or after school in addition to your training sessions will need to be accounted for by you as a coach.
- A good *demonstration and explanation* of the drill, alongside a clear indication of the coaching points, will save time and

will speed up the learning process. Have a maximum of two or three coaching points to emphasize the drill you run – keep it short and simple and straight to the point so that players understand what they have to do. Corrections, feedback, praise, encouragement – all these need to be part of the coach repertoire when running drills! Constant emphasis on the coaching points is an aspect that coaches operating at all levels of the game need to focus on while delivering and teaching a new drill/new skill. And make sure you allow plenty of time for repetitions so that players actually get a chance to put in practice what you want them to learn. Fig. 1 tries to summarize these key points and general considerations that need to be taken into account when coaching.

- When using drills do not be afraid to immediately (as soon as you see something) correct players when they are making mistakes and, equally, do not be afraid to praise players when they succeed in doing what you ask them to do. In relation to this, a good idea might be to encourage your players to learn auto-correction as a skill – develop your players so that they learn and know the coaching points and how to auto-correct themselves when the coach is not watching!

- The discussion about the role of the coach is not necessarily the focus of this book; however, providing corrections and making sure players do not practise bad habits is a central and a major part of this role. The idea of providing high level(s) of corrections and frequent provision of feedback (verbal, video and written) has been highlighted in the coaching literature numerous times – to support this point and to get more info, see the work of Cross and Lyle (2002) and Doug and Hastie (1993) as some of the most relevant examples, amongst others. All this, in combination with the above-mentioned

instruction, demonstration and so on, will lead to what Cross and Lyle (2002) define as coach and coaching effectiveness – in this way you as a coach will be effective in your attempts to coach!

'When?' and 'why?' – it is so important that players understand the reasons why we ask them to practise certain moves during the training and also in what context and when. This will allow them to make better decisions once they master the particular move and definitely during games, when the time pressure is obvious as is the pressure from the defenders.

- Apart from this, *questioning* as an approach to coaching is highly advisable, especially when delivering information – this is a skill in itself and should be part of a coach's skillset.

- As an element of good practice, try to give a name to a drill when it is used so that players remember it easily for next time (hopefully!). This will avoid wasting time by repeating explanation and demonstration, and will lead to the creation of team habits, players attitudes and so on.

- Making the drills as close as possible to some of your team's play, to your offensive actions (or defensive actions) will help a lot with the application of these actions from the training into the games.

- Avoid just a simple 'copy and paste' approach when introducing a new drill and generally when allowing skill learning to happen. Coaches in basketball and other sports will learn from other coaches, and will implement elements in their training drills that they see elsewhere. While there are plenty of benefits in this, the simple 'copy and paste' approach can be a dangerous one – ideally when you see a new drill this needs to be adapted and possibly slightly modified to suit your particular needs and the context in which you operate with regards to level and ability of

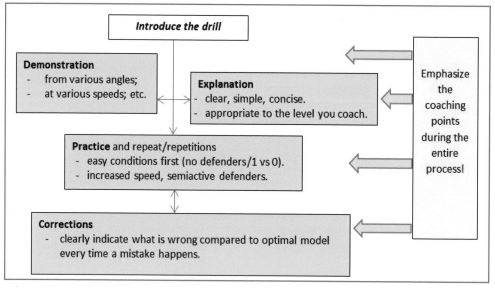

Fig. 1 Considerations when introducing a new drill/new skill (authors' own elaboration).

own players, moment in time during the season, resources available and so on.

- As a coach, when planning your training session, make sure you have two or three options for a particular drill just in case you plan for twelve players and only nine players show up to training. The same thing applies in the case of some participants learning a bit quicker while others learn slower – being organized and well prepared will be very helpful in these situations.

INDIVIDUALIZATION

Certain principles of training need to be taken into account when creating a training programme. In his earlier work, Radu (2015) highlights the fact that *individualization* appears as one of the most important training principles listed by various authors (see for example Pike, 2001; Sports Coach UK, 2007; Beeching, 2011), alongside multilateral development, specificity, progression, reversibility, variety and recovery. It is 'an essential element of the

coaching process' as Cross considers (Cross, 2002, cited in Cross and Lyle, 2002). As a coach, you need to control the 'controllables' where this is possible (aspects such as what goes into a session plan, how long you practise, with defence or with no defence) while other aspects are determined by the athlete themselves and/or the environment you operate within. In a basketball squad you have twelve to fourteen (or even more) individuals who all will present differences in terms of height, body size and shape, speed, agility, balance, co-ordination, psychological preferences and so on. Your training approach should be orientated towards the team, while keeping in mind that most of the things you do need to be specific to the individuals who are part of the team. The difficulty arises when players have a particular preference for a specific position. This is a situation that the coach needs to manage sensibly, discussing with the athlete and highlighting clearly the requirements of each of the positions on court (while looking at the skills assessment of the player involved).

Individualization can create problems in team sports such as basketball because of the various constraints – for example time, as not all the players will be free at specific times (during the mornings for example) due to school commitments as is the case with junior basketball, or sports hall availability, or the lack of enough training time for the team and so on. Getting your athletes to understand that they need to do extra work might be a solution and a specific, individualized plan (training programme) can be created by the coach, for example work on their shooting technique; practise their defensive moves or improve their overall general fitness. This situation requires an element of trust in the sense that when given instructions, the player will actually carry them out! This trust is obviously more easily established with more advanced players. Co-operation between the two parties involved (coach and athlete) is clearly necessary in order to achieve the mutual goal – for the athlete to get better and improve their game. Apart from techniques and tactics, other areas such as sport psychology, physiotherapy, nutrition and performance analysis need to be incorporated into an individualized training programme and this is where the coach will have a major say in the creation and the content of this programme.

This principle of individualization (or individuality) will allow coaches to identify drills and exercises and coaches will have to adapt these to the individual characteristics of each player (such as age; gender; playing ability; level of experience and years of training or personality type) and to their specific needs, and this will be done while addressing specific areas of preparation such as technical preparation, tactical preparation, physical preparation and so on. Most of the drills presented in the following chapters – drills with and without a ball, drills performed individually or in pairs and in small groups – will help coaches to apply this principle in practice.

PART 1

DRILLS FOR SPECIFIC PLAYING POSITIONS

2 | DRILLS FOR GUARDS

In terms of terminology, the guard position is usually subdivided into point guard and shooting guard, and there are some differences between the roles and characteristics of these two posts. 'Playmaker' is another term that is used mainly in European basketball and it indicates a guard, a point guard more specifically – as the name suggests the main responsibility for this player is to make the play(s), in other words to get the team organized and to run the show when the team is playing. That would include announcing and running the plays (see Fig. 2 for an example of a player indicating the play that the team will run), bringing and advancing the ball up the floor for the offensive moments and implementing the defensive strategy of the team. Lots of coaches refer to this player as 'the floor general' because in effect this player is the general who is organizing the 'troops' (all other four players who are on the court at the same time) or as 'the coach on the court'.

Guards need to be the level-headed player in the team, constantly focused on what the game and what the opposition will provide. They will bring an element of leadership into the equation because they must lead the team while on the court. Self-control is probably the essential personal characteristic for any player that wants to fulfil the requirements of this post – when your 'commander' is calm and in control, this is when the team has a chance to execute the game plan and to win the game. Communication ability has to be well above the average of the team. Considering the fact that they hold the ball most of the time (more than any other player does), dribbling and passing with high levels of efficiency and accuracy are two of the most important basketball skills they need to possess. The point guards are very much team-orientated players – they need to create chances for others and this is when the ability to pass and share the ball and send the assist is paramount in their skills repertoire. These are followed by a good shooting ability – when the opportunity to take the shot comes, they need to be ready; this applies to the shooting guard in particular as lots of teams will rely on this player when it comes to who is taking the shot no matter if it is a long-range shot, mid-range or close to basket. High levels of energy will enable the guards to be disruptive in defence and force the opposition into making turnovers. Other essential personal attributes for the guards are memory and decision-making; they need to know and remember all the plays that their own team runs. On the top of this, a great

17

Fig. 2 Playmaker who indicates the play that the team will run.

guard also learns the plays that the opposite teams are running, and this will help them to prepare for a specific opponent so that when they play against them they hold a slight advantage. Lastly, court awareness and court vision will help them exploit the weaknesses of opponents and will maximize their own team strengths.

DRIBBLE FORWARDS AND BACKWARDS AND ATTACK THE BASKET DRILL

Description: One player at a time will dribble the ball with their right hand, forward from the halfway line up to just being level with the cone. Using a continuous dribble with the same hand, they will now use a retreat dribble (dribble backwards) using two to three dribbles (*see* Fig. 3). At this point they will use a crossover move and change their dribbling hand, now dribbling inside and attacking the cone that is situated above the free throw line.

Here they will use another crossover move after which they will take a final dribble with the right hand and take a lay-up (right-hand lay-up).

Use/purpose: The drill can be used as a warm-up drill but also as part of the individualization process for guards. The overall aim is to develop ball control (while dribbling with both hands forwards/backwards) and also ability to finish at the basket.

Materials and equipment required: One ball per player; one basket/hoop (ideally on a half court) and two cones.

Coaching points: Players need to be encouraged to:

- Keep their head up when dribbling.
- Change their dribbling hand after each of the two changes of direction (in front of the cones).
- Keep the ball at the same level with their hips (or slightly behind) when dribbling backwards.
- Powerfully attack the basket on the last dribble to take the lay-up.

PROGRESSION:

- Instead of a crossover move, use a dribble between the legs, behind the back dribble or spin dribble (360 degrees).
- After a few reps on the right-hand side, do the same on the left-hand side and finish with left-hand lay-up.

- Take a reverse lay-up instead of a lay-up (*see* Fig. 4).
- Take a jump shot instead of a lay-up (*see* Fig. 5).
- Use a semiactive defender instead of the cone that is close to the sideline.

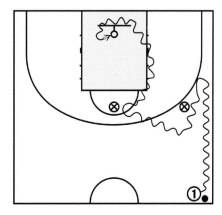

Fig. 4 Dribble forwards and backwards and attack the basket drill – with reverse lay-up.

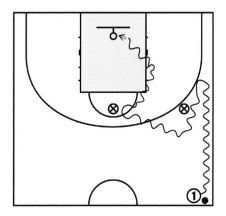

Fig. 3 Dribble forwards and backwards and attack the basket drill (with lay-up).

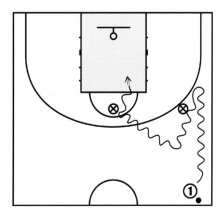

Fig. 5 Dribble forwards and backwards and attack the basket drill – with a jump shot.

DRIBBLE PAST THE CONE, ATTACK THE DEFENDER AND TAKE A JUMP SHOT DRILL

Description: From the central circle, player 1 will start dribbling with their right hand towards the closest cone (*see* Fig. 6). Once in front of the cone, they will continue the dribble with the same hand, 'beating' the cone (which could be a passive defender). After another dribble, they will perform a crossover move when close to the cone that is on the right-hand side and after one dribble with the left hand they will catch and shoot from around the free throw line. The

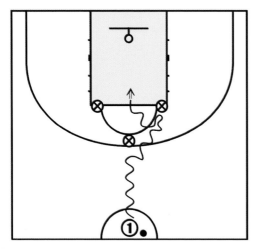
Fig. 6 Dribble past the cone drill.

player can start the drill with their left hand and then do the same using their left hand.

Use/purpose: To develop the ability to dribble against a defender and the ability to take a jump shot (off the dribble). Also, it allows players to work on dribbling with either hand.

Materials and equipment required: One ball per player; one basket/hoop (ideally on a half court) and three cones.

Coaching points: Players need to be encouraged to:

• Take a good, well-balanced shot, and to follow through (leave the arm extended after the shot).

• To keep their head up when dribbling and when changing the dribbling hand after the crossover move.

• When attacking the first cone, try to protect the ball and keep it away from the cone (from the defender). When dribbling with the right hand, use the left arm and left foot to protect the ball (*see* Fig. 7)

Fig. 7 Player who protects the ball with their hand and foot.

PROGRESSION:

- Use a dribble between the legs instead of a crossover, then behind the back or a 360-degrees move.
- Use a fake before taking a shot.
- Use a semiactive defender instead of the cone at the top of the 3 points semicircle.
- Use a hesitation dribble and go round the second cone to take the jump shot instead of crossover move/inside move (*see* Fig. 8).

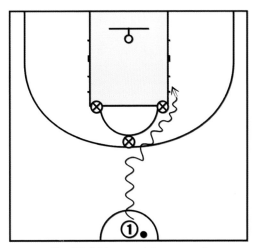

Fig. 8 Dribble passed the cone and take a jump shot drill.

SPACING GAME BETWEEN GUARD AND GUARD – DRIBBLE AND PASS TO THE CUTTING PLAYER DRILL

Description: From a two guards set-up, player 1 will dribble the ball sideline–baseline as if they will go to the basket and take a lay-up. At the same time, player 2 will cut towards the opposite side of the court – around the short corner area – as illustrated in Fig. 9. Player 1 will take three to four dribbles maximum, and when arriving close to the basket will pass the ball to player 2 who will catch and shoot.

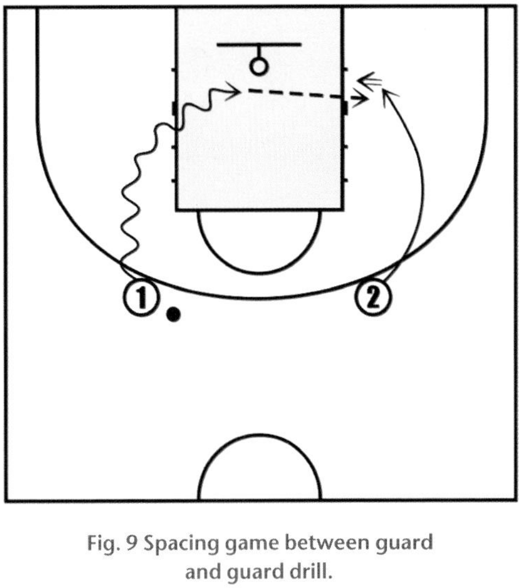

Use/purpose: The drill develops passing ability and the vision of the player playing guard position (see the open teammate). At the same time it develops the ability to read the game (for player 2 in particular). Catch and shoot is also being practised.

Materials and equipment required: One ball between two players; one hoop/basket (ideally on a half court); possibly some markers or mats on court to signal the initial starting points.

Coaching points: Players need to be encouraged to:

- Attack the basket with a powerful, convincing dribble while keeping their head up.
- Send a powerful pass to their teammate.
- Synchronize their moves – do not cut to the basket too early before or too late after the dribbling action starts.
- Have their hands ready to receive the pass so that they can catch and shoot (*see* Fig. 10).

Fig. 9 Spacing game between guard and guard drill.

Fig. 10 Player who has their hands ready to receive and catch the ball.

Fig. 11 Player who sends a one-hand pass to a teammate.

PROGRESSION:

- Use one hand only when sending the pass, as in Fig. 11.
- Use/limit the number of dribbles to a maximum of two to three before passing.
- The player who cuts will get open for a 3 points shot.
- Player 1 starts the drill by dribbling towards the middle/inside of the court while player 2 will move/cut towards the free throw line extended, as in Fig. 12.
- Player 2 has the option to catch and shoot but the coach can add some additional elements such as: catch – fake (shooting fake) – one dribble and shoot the ball (shoot off the dribble).

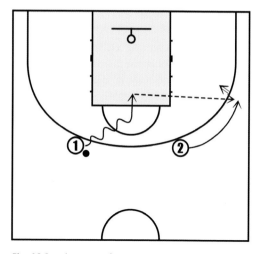

Fig. 12 Spacing game between guard and guard with dribble towards the middle drill.

SPACING GAME BETWEEN GUARD AND GUARD – DRIBBLE AND PASS TO TEAMMATE WHO REPLACES YOU

Description: From a two-guard set up, player 1 dribbles the ball sideline–baseline towards the basket (in a similar manner to the previous drill). When the dribbling action starts, player 2 will replace the space occupied by player 1 – player 2 will cut towards that area of the court (*see* Fig. 13). After two to three dribbles, player 1 will stop their drive to the basket and will pass to player 2, who will catch and shoot.

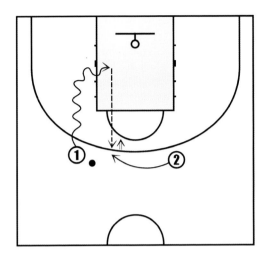

Fig. 13 Spacing game between guard and guard –
with player who replaces teammate drill.

Use/purpose: The guard with the ball practises their dribbling and passing ability, while developing their court vision. Player 2 develops their ability to read the game, and also their catch and shoot ability.

Materials and equipment required: One ball between two players; one hoop/basket (ideally on a half court); possibly some markers or mats on court to signal the initial starting points.

Coaching points: Players need to be encouraged to:

- Attack the basket with a powerful, convincing dribble while keeping their head up.
- Send a powerful pass to their teammate.
- Synchronize their moves – do not cut to the basket too early before or too late after the dribbling action starts.
- Have their hands ready to receive the pass so that they can catch and shoot.

PROGRESSION:

- Use one hand only when sending the pass.
- Use/limit the number of dribbles to a maximum of two to three before passing.
- Add some additional elements for player 2 such as: catch – fake (shooting fake) – one dribble and shoot the ball (shoot off the dribble).
- Modify the starting point for player 2 (see Fig. 14). Player 2 starts from the corner of the court on the same side as player 1. This time player 1 will start dribbling towards the inside of the court (towards the middle of the key). When dribbling action starts, player 2 will replace the space where 1 started from. Player 1 will stop the dribble and reverse the ball to 2, who will catch and shoot.

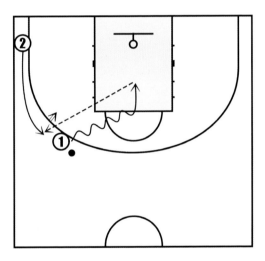

Fig. 14 Spacing game between guard and guard –
with non-dribbling player starting on the corner.

DRIBBLE AGAINST PRESSURE AND DRIVE TO THE BASKET DRILL

Description: Player 1 with the ball will start in the central circle of the court, while three defenders are positioned as shown in Fig. 15 (two on the right and one on the left side).

Player 1 will start dribbling with their right hand towards the area between the two stationary defenders. When the attacker is about 1–2m away, the two defenders will initiate an

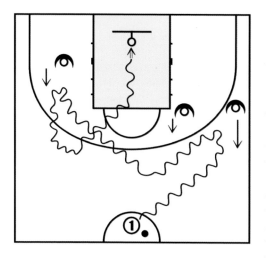

Fig. 15 Dribble against pressure and drive to the basket drill.

action towards player 1 as if they would trap this attacker, with arms wide open, using a defensive stance position/move (*see* Fig. 16). When defenders approach them, player 1 will dribble backwards two to three times using a retreat dribble, so that they keep possession while dribbling, and will use a crossover move in order to 'escape' and dribble away from the two defenders, who now will stop their forwards moving action – they are now dribbling using their left hand towards the individual defender on the left. Once approaching them, the defender will apply pressure on the ball in a semiactive manner (they will start defending the ball approaching the ball handler), forcing the attacker to use another two to three retreat dribbles and then, following another crossover

Fig. 16 Attacking player with ball who is guarded by two defenders.

dribble, the attacking player will dribble/drive all the way to the basket in order to take a lay-up (unguarded lay-up).

Use/purpose: The drill develops dribbling ability against pressure (the pressure from one or two defenders) and allows the attacker to take a quick decision while dribbling. From a defensive point of view – it gets the defenders to work together and stop the drive.

Materials and equipment required: One ball; one basket (preferably on a half court).

Coaching points: Players need to be encouraged to:

• Always keep their head up when dribbling, irrespective of direction, forwards, backwards or sideways (*see* Fig. 17).

• Protect the ball and control it all the time.
• Defenders – use a low stance and get both arms out when stopping the dribbler.

PROGRESSION:

• Take a jump shot instead of a lay-up at the end of the drill.
• After the second retreat dribble, the drill can become 'live' and the attacking player starts playing 1 vs 1 live with the defender on that part of the court.

Fig. 17 Player with the ball who keeps their head up when dribbling.

3 DRILLS FOR FORWARDS

Exactly as with the guards, the forward position can be put into two sub-categories: small forwards and power forwards. Athleticism is the main physical attribute for these players; apart from this, they can run the floor, can hustle in defence (they are generally some of the better defenders in the team) and can also shoot the ball consistently well. Rebounding is another component that is present in their game (mainly for the power forward but also for the small forward) as well as boxing out (*see* Fig. 18) – in this way they are able to use their size (height) and strength in order to get the ball and also to help teammates get open.

Fig. 18 The players in light vests are boxing out their opponents.

GET OPEN, RECEIVE THE BALL AND ATTACK THE BASKET DRILL

Description: The whole group is positioned on court as shown in Fig. 19. Players 1 and 6 have a ball each. Player 1 will start dribbling with the left hand across the court towards player 4, who is on the opposite wing. As soon as the dribble starts, player 4 will perform a V cut by going away from the ball towards the corner of the court and coming/sprinting to the initial spot to meet the ball from player 1, who will pass after performing three to four dribbles max. After receiving the ball, player 4 will square to the basket using a pivoting action so that they face the basket, and will dribble towards the basket in order to take a lay-up. They will then collect their own rebound and join the end of the opposite queue. Player 1 now becomes the next player on that wing who will get open (after a V cut) and player 1 will receive the ball from player 2, who will continue the drill. As soon as player 1 starts the drill, player 6 will take exactly the same action towards the opposite basket, dribble with their right hand and pass to player 5, who will get open and will take a lay-up, and so on.

Use/purpose: The drill develops the ability to get open on the wing (at a 45-degree angle) where the forward usually plays. It enhances the dribbling skills and passing to a teammate on time (timing of the pass).

Materials and equipment required: Minimum four balls; one court with two hoops. Minimum six to eight players or more.

Coaching points: Players need to be encouraged to:

- Get open properly by jogging 4–5m away from the ball and then sprinting to receive the ball.
- Have their arms ready to catch the ball.
- Dribble with their head up, trying to send a well-timed pass to their teammate (not too early, not too late!).
- Finish strong at the basket.

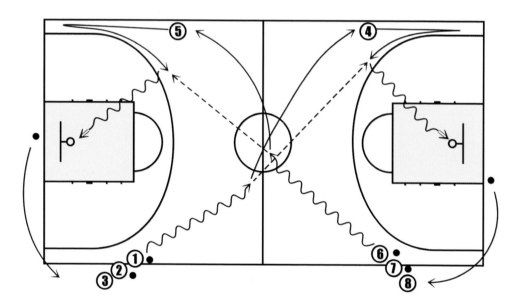

Fig. 19 Get open, receive the ball and attack the basket drill.

PROGRESSION:

- After catching the ball on the wing, players can use a fake followed by one quick dribble and take a jump shot. Players should avoid dribbling in front of the legs – they should try to do it diagonally forward or sideways.

- As a coach, you can get the whole group to score ten or more consecutive times when taking the lay-ups before moving to the next drill. If a lay-up is missed, the whole group goes back to zero.
- Player 1 can send a pass to player 4, who will perform a back door cut after the initial V cut (*see* Fig. 20).

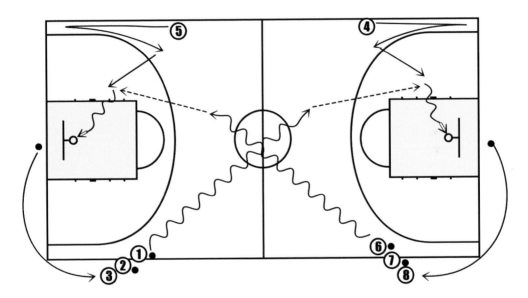

Fig. 20 Get open, receive the ball and attack the basket drill – with back door cut option.

CURL CUT, RECEIVE AND LAY-UP DRILL

Description: The group of players is positioned as indicated in Fig. 21. Player 1 who starts the drill does not have a ball, while players 2, 3, 5 and 6 will have a ball each. Player 1 will perform a cut to the basket followed by a curl cut around the cone at the top of the key. This is when 1 will receive the pass from player 5, and then 1 will dribble with their right hand to take the right-hand lay-up. After passing to 1, player 5 will continue the drill by performing a similar move and after receiving from 2, will take a lay-up with their left hand (*see* Fig. 22). And the drill continues following a similar pattern.

Use/purpose: It develops the ability to use a curl cut towards the basket, to pass accurately to a teammate and to finish strong to the basket. This can be used as a competitive warming-up drill if/when performed by two groups of players (minimum six to eight in each group) with one group at one basket and the other one at the opposite end.

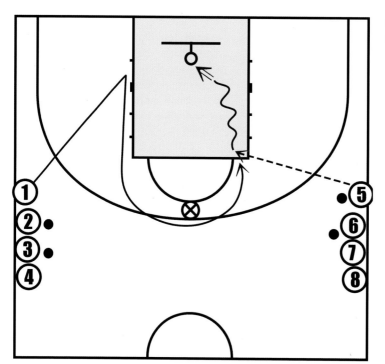

Fig. 21 Curl cut, receive and lay-up drill.

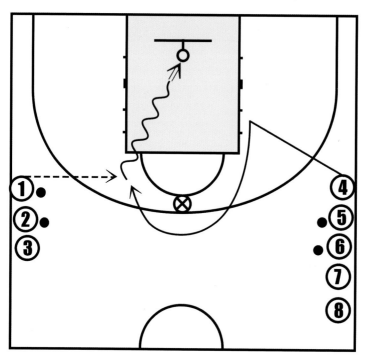

Fig. 22 Curl cut, receive and lay-up drill (continuation for the drill).

Materials and equipment required: Four balls; one cone (a chair could be used); one basket on a half court.

Coaching points: Players need to be encouraged to:

- Cut powerfully to the basket after going round the cone and have their arms ready to receive the pass.
- When getting open, try to have one foot in the paint and then sprint to meet the ball.
- Be ready to pass when they are at the front of the queue – on time and accurately!

PROGRESSION:

- Once the ball has been received, catch and shoot from the elbow area.
- Player 1 can perform a back door cut after the initial V cut (*see* Fig. 23). In this situation player 5 will send a lob pass (a slightly higher pass as if it would go over a few defenders in the middle of the key) and then player 1 will catch and shoot from close to the basket.

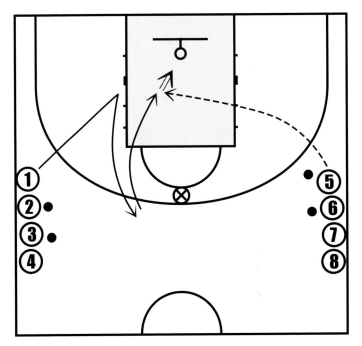

Fig. 23 Curl cut, receive and lay-up drill – with back door cut option.

PASS TO WING, CUT AND REPLACE DRILL (WITH NO DRIBBLE)

Description: In groups of three, players are positioned in a one guard and two forwards set-up as illustrated in Fig. 24. Player 1 has the ball and will pass to player 2. After passing, player 1 will cut to the basket and will go to the corner that is opposite to the ball. As soon as player 1 leaves their spot and starts their cut, player 3 will replace player 1, who, after going to the corner initially, will replace the spot that player 3 had at the start of the drill. This is when player 2 (who now has the ball) will pass to player 3 at the top and 3 will immediately pass to 1 on the opposite wing (*see* Fig. 25). The drill continues with player 3

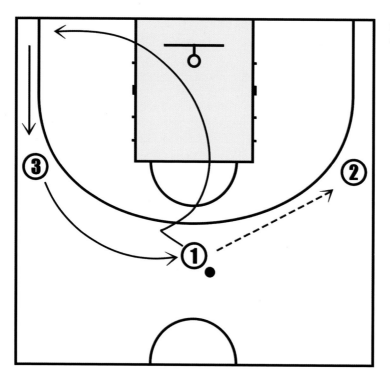

Fig. 24 Pass to wing, cut and replace drill.

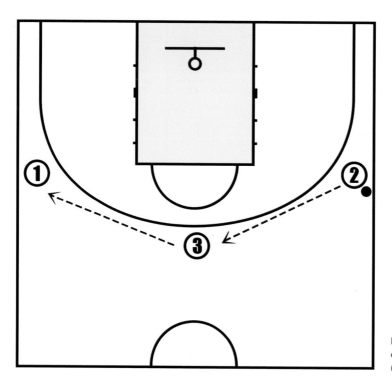

Fig. 25 Pass to wing, cut and replace drill (continuation).

who will now cut towards the basket as if they want to receive the ball and will eventually move to the opposite corner without actually receiving the ball during their cut (*see* Fig. 26). The drill continues following a similar pattern with the ball moving from side to side and players passing and cutting to the basket.

Use/purpose: A very useful drill for developing playing without the ball ability (especially cut and replace actions) while knowing what their teammates are doing on court. It also works on passing ability and on switching the play from side to side, as it happens when player 1 passes to player 2 and then immediately to player 3 – from one wing to the other.

Materials and equipment required: One ball between three players; one basket on a half court.

Coaching points: Players need to be encouraged to:

- Make sure they 'show their hands' every time they cut towards the basket – have their arms out in front ready to catch the ball (*see* Fig. 27).
- When catching the ball, make sure they square up to the basket (pivot so that they end up facing the basket and become a threat).
- Send a strong, powerful chest pass to teammates.

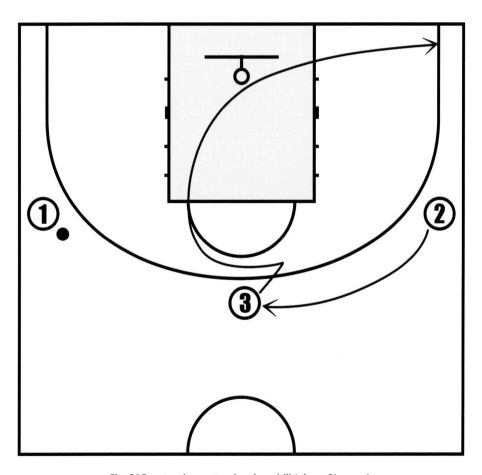

Fig. 26 Pass to wing, cut and replace drill (player 3's move).

Fig. 27 Player who shows their hands when cutting to the basket.

PROGRESSION:
- Before every catch, they should try to get open, using a V cut or an L cut
- Add a passive or semiactive defender into the drill.

- Play 3 vs 3 live after a minimum of four to five passes. It can be left as a free game or you can use a restriction, such as only one dribble allowed.

SPACING IN THREE PLAYERS WITH DRIBBLING FROM THE WING DRILL

Description: Three players are positioned as in Fig. 28 – one guard and two forwards set up. Player 1 who has the ball will drive (dribble) towards the basket (towards the middle of the court). This is when players 2 and 3 will cut to a new spot on the court: player 3 will go to the nearest corner of the court while player 2 will replace player 3 (will go to occupy their spot). The aim of the drill is for player 1 to pass to one of their teammates who will catch and shoot – for example, if the pass goes to player 3, they will shoot as illustrated in Fig. 29.

Use/purpose: This is a very effective drill that teaches players how to play without the ball and how to move on the court when a team-mate dribbles the ball. Dribbling and passing ability (finding their teammate) will also be improved while being spaced out on the court (4–5m apart). Good as a warm-up activity (in a competition format for example) but also as content in the main part of a session.

Materials and equipment required: One ball between three players; one basket on a half court.

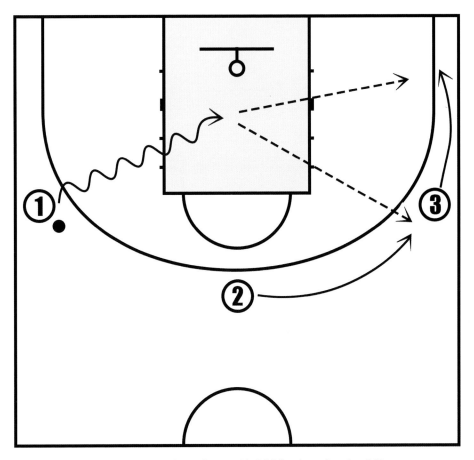

Fig. 28 Spacing in three players with dribbling from the wing drill.

Coaching points: Players need to be encouraged to:

- For the two players who do not have the ball – keep an eye on their teammate who will dribble, and not to cut too early or too late to their new spot.
- Keep their head up when dribbling.
- Send a good, strong, powerful pass. For more advanced players, get them to try a one-hand pass.
- Be ready to receive the ball as soon as they move to a new spot.

PROGRESSION:

- Player 1 drives sideline–baseline while player 2 will replace player 1 (instead of 2 replacing 3). Player 3 will do as before: go to the corner (*see* Fig. 30).
- Add a semiactive defender who will guard player 1.
- Add a semiactive defender on either player 2 or 3 and ask player 1 to pass to the unguarded teammate.
- Make sure you rotate players to a new starting spot and remind them to go and rebound if they are not shooting.

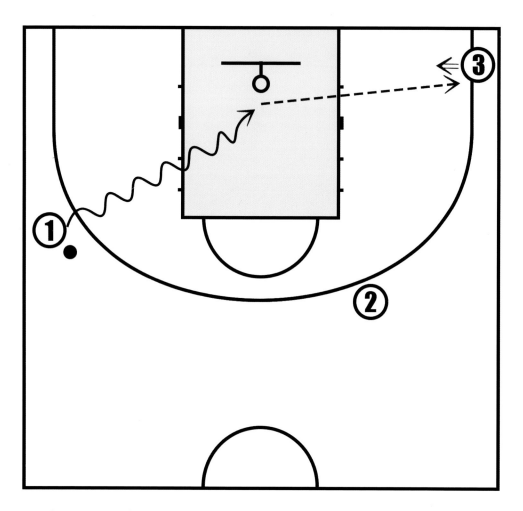

Fig. 29 Spacing in three players with dribbling from the wing drill – with player 3 taking the shot.

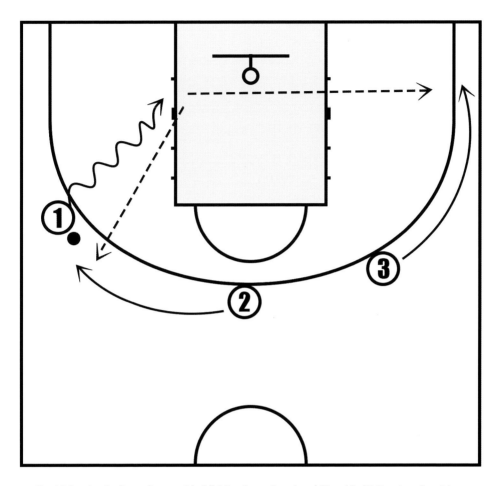

Fig. 30 Spacing in three players with dribbling from the wing drill – with sideline–baseline drive.

SPACING IN THREE PLAYERS WITH DRIBBLE FROM THE TOP DRILL

Description: Initial set-up for the drill is one guard and two forwards. Player 1 (guard) has the ball and they will start the drill by dribbling either side of the cone in order to go to the basket. This is when forwards 2 and 3 will cut to the corner on the side of the court they are on, so that player 1 has two options for a pass (*see* Fig. 31). After two to three dribbles, player 1 will pass the ball to one of the two teammates who will shoot, trying to score.

Use/purpose: A very good warm-up drill (competitive conditions could also be employed – have two groups, one group at each basket) but also as the content during the main part of the session so that players learn/ practise/refine movement on court when they do not have the ball. Passing, dribbling, catch and shoot are all being practised while spacing out on the court and while responding to a move from the teammate with the ball.

Materials and equipment required: One ball between three players; one cone; one basket on a half court.

Coaching points: Players need to be encouraged to:

- Keep their head up when dribbling.
- Send a good powerful pass to their teammate.
- Have their hands ready to receive after they move to a new spot.

PROGRESSION:

- For more advanced players – one-hand pass to be used.

- Add a passive or semiactive defender on player 1 (instead of a cone).
- Make sure you rotate players to a new starting spot and remind them to go and rebound if they are not shooting.
- Add a semiactive defender on either player 2 or 3 and ask player 1 to pass to the unguarded teammate.
- Instead of going to the corner, player 2 can replace player 1 (see Fig. 32).

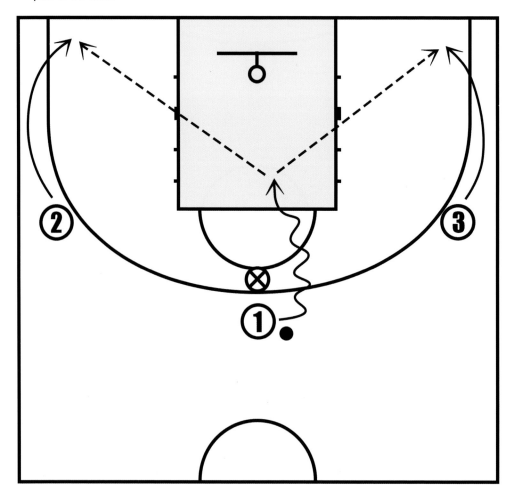

Fig. 31 Spacing in three players with dribble from the top drill.

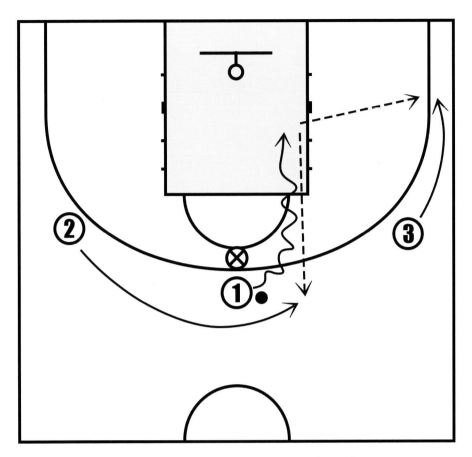

Fig. 32 Spacing in three players – with player 2 replacing player 1.

SPACING IN FOUR PLAYERS WITH DRIBBLE FROM THE TOP DRILL

Description: Four players are positioned on the court as in Fig. 33 with a two guards and two forwards set-up. Player 2 with the ball will start the drill and will dribble to the basket. This is when players 1, 3 and 4 will cut/move to a new spot: player 1 will go to the corner, same for player 4, while player 3 will replace the position that was occupied by player 4. After two to three dribbles, player 2 will pass the ball to one of their teammates who will take the shot – for example in Fig. 34, player 2 passes to player 3, and 3 will shoot.

Use/purpose: The drill develops timing and co-ordination of actions following a pre-established pattern when a teammate dribbles the ball. Also passing, catch and shoot, movement without the ball and spacing – all these fundamental actions are being practised.

Materials and equipment required: One ball for four players; one basket on a half court.

Coaching points: Players need to be encouraged to:

- Keep their head up when dribbling.
- Send a good powerful pass to their teammate.

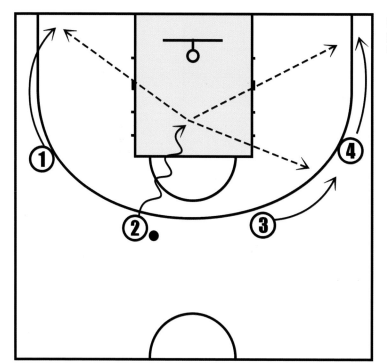

Fig. 33 Spacing in four players with dribble from the top drill.

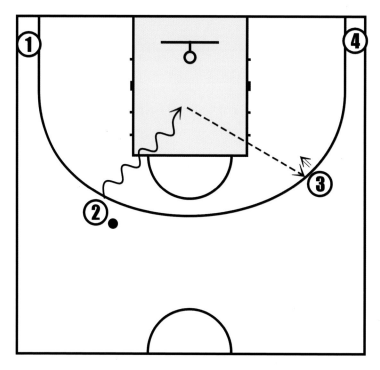

Fig. 34 Spacing in four players with dribble from the top and player 3 taking the shot.

- Have their hands ready to receive after they move to a new spot.

PROGRESSION:

- Add a passive (and then semiactive) defender to guard player 2.

- Add another defender on any other player on court – and the pass needs to go to any of the two other players who are not guarded.

- Player 1 and/or 3 can replace player 2 (*see* Fig. 35).

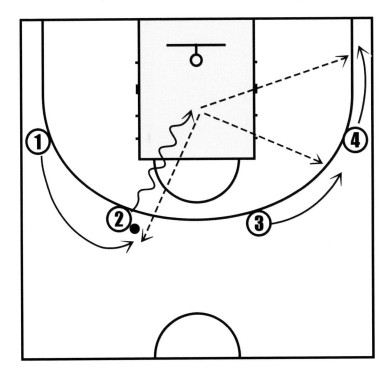

Fig. 35 Spacing in four players with dribble from the top and player 1 (or 3) replacing player 2.

SPACING IN FOUR PLAYERS WITH DRIBBLE FROM THE CORNER DRILL

Description: Four players are positioned as in Fig. 36 – player 1 with the ball is positioned in the corner, players 2, 3 and 4 around the 3 points semicircle (spaced out in a one guard, two forwards set-up). Player 1 will dribble the ball towards the basket as if they intend to go and score a lay-up. At the same time as the first dribble, the other three players will move at the same time as follows: player 4 goes to the corner, player 3 will replace and take the spot occupied initially by 4 while player 2 will replace 3. Player 1 has a choice of three potential teammates to pass to. The player who receives the ball will catch and shoot – for example in Fig. 37 player 3 will receive, and will catch and shoot.

Use/purpose: The drill develops timing and co-ordination of players' actions following a pre-established pattern when a teammate dribbles the ball. Also, passing, catch and shoot, movement without the ball and spacing – all these fundamental actions are being practised.

Materials and equipment required: One ball for four players; one basket on a half court.

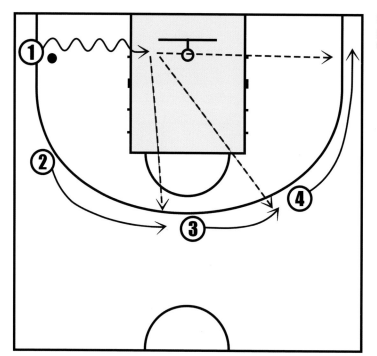

Fig. 36 Spacing in four players with dribble from the corner drill.

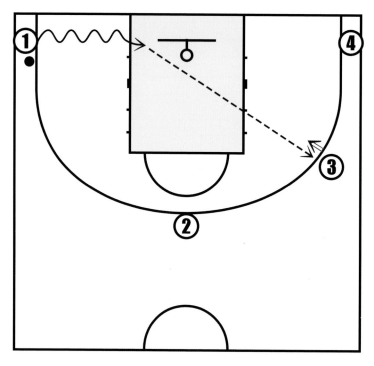

Fig. 37 Spacing in four players with dribble from the corner drill with player 3 shooting.

Coaching points: Players need to be encouraged to:

- Keep their head up when dribbling.
- Send a good powerful pass to their teammate.
- Have their hands ready to receive after they move to a new spot.
- Go and get the rebound after the shot is taken.

PROGRESSION:

- Add a semiactive defender on player 1.
- Add another defender on any other player on court – and the pass needs to go to any of the two other players who are not guarded.
- Players 2 and 3 can move onto a new direction and replace the corresponding player from that area (*see* Fig. 38).

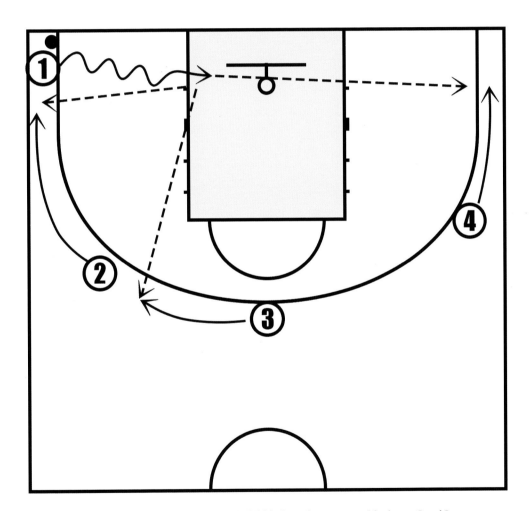

Fig. 38 Spacing in four players with dribble from the corner – with players 2 and 3 replacing the corresponding player.

4 | DRILLS FOR CENTRES

Playing in the post, close to the basket, requires certain skills and abilities apart from just being a tall or indeed a very tall player (which is actually the major advantage for this type of player). Centres will usually use parts of their body to their advantage – upper body to protect the ball; knees and legs to be strong and well-balanced in the battle with other centres/players and also to occupy a good position close to the basket; arms to block shots (*see* Fig. 39) and to collect rebounds; whole body to set screens for teammates (*see*

Fig. 39 A centre who is blocking a shot.

Fig. 40 and Fig. 41) and also to box out and keep attackers away from their own basket.

In terms of some of the main responsibilities for centres we can include: rebounding, both defensive and offensive (*see* Fig. 42); defending the basket (some centres are called the 'rim protector'); setting screens for teammates in offence and boxing out opposition players. If in the past centres were limited with regards to their basketball skills, in recent years they have developed their skills and there are now centres who can dribble the ball and who can shoot mid-range, in some cases even long-range shots too. Low post and high post are the main areas of the court where they operate. Also, it is worth remembering that they will get fouled a lot and because of this, their ability to score free throws is essential.

Fig. 41 A screen set by the centre with their back towards the player who will be screened.

Fig. 42 A centre who rebounds the ball.

Fig. 40 A screen set by a centre (player in light vest on the right) while facing the player who is going to be screened.

SKIP PASS, CUT FROM WEAK SIDE AND FINISH AT THE BASKET DRILL

Description: Player 5 (centre) is positioned in the low post area (just outside the key) with their back to the basket, facing towards the sideline, as in Fig. 43. They have a ball and will start the drill by sending a skip pass to a coach (or passing player) who is on the opposite wing (free throw line extended). Once the coach has received the ball, player 5 will initiate a move towards the middle of the key (round the cone) and will cut in order to receive the pass from the coach. On the catch (somewhere in front of the basket), player 5 will take a shot from very close to the basket with the right hand in this instance (after every three to four turns doing the same move, try and use a variety of shots such as hook shot, semihook shot or

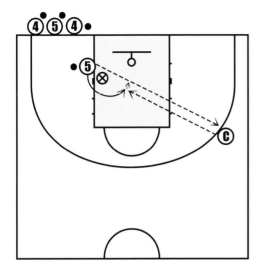

Fig. 43 Skip pass, cut from weak side and finish at the basket drill.

up and under move). Once player 5 has finished the shot, they will either take their own rebound (and shoot again to score) or collect the ball after a made basket and will join the queue on the baseline and the drill continues with the next player – 4 in this instance – who will have their turn, and so on.

Use/purpose: The drill develops the ability to play with the back to the basket. It is also used to practise a skip pass (strong, powerful pass from low post to the opposite wing). Lastly, it is useful to practise a variety of shots and moves for the centre around and close to the basket area.

Materials and equipment required: One ball per player; one basket on a half court (with clearly visible court markings).

Coaching points: Players need to be encouraged to:

- From an initial post up position (*see* Fig. 44 for a good position with the ball in both hands) send a strong, powerful pass to the opposite wing.

- Cut strongly to the basket and 'ask for the ball' with at least one hand but preferably both hands up towards the ball (*see* Fig. 45).

Fig. 44 Post player (centre) with ball in both hands in the low post area after he received a pass and is ready to play.

Fig. 45 Post player 'asking' for the ball from teammates.

- Go and collect their own rebound if the shot is missed and put it back in order to score.
- Whatever type of shot they take (for example jump shot, hook shot, semihook shot, up and under move, drop step towards the baseline, drop step towards the middle), make sure they execute it properly (follow through, well-balanced, paying attention to rules such as travel).

PROGRESSION:

- Alternate the type of shot that is being taken: for example catch and shoot using a hook shot; a semihook shot; catch and jump off two feet and shoot; up and under move, drop step towards the baseline or drop step towards the middle. A quick powerful dribble can then be added, such as catch, one dribble and up/take the shot or catch, one dribble and use a spin move to finish with a shot with the left hand.
- Start the drill from the other side and finish with a left-hand shot (*see* Fig. 46).

- Add a semiactive defender on player 5 who will maintain a presence in defence without actually trying to block the shot.

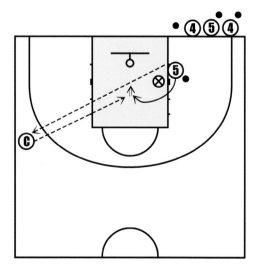

Fig. 46 Skip pass, cut from weak side and finish at the basket with left-hand shot drill.

PASS, CUT, RECEIVE, DRIBBLE AND SHOOT DRILL FOR CENTRES

Description: Player 5 (who has a ball) starts the drill from the central circle of the court, facing the basket that they will attack and will send a pass to the coach (or to a passing player) and then will cut towards the basket. The coach will return the pass so that player 5 will receive the ball around the free throw line area, on the right elbow (high post area). After the catch, player 5 will perform a shooting fake, then will take one or two powerful dribbles followed by a two steps lay-up with right-hand finish. They will collect their own ball and join the back of the queue as seen in Fig. 47. Player 4 will be the next one to continue the drill.

Use/purpose: The drill develops the ability to play while facing the basket. It encourages players to cut to high post area and use a fake before taking a shot. Finishing strong at the basket is another aim for this drill. Can be used as warm up or during the individualization sessions.

Materials and equipment required: One ball per player; one basket on a half court.

Coaching points: Players need to be encouraged to:
- Send a powerful pass to the coach or a passing player.
- Use a convincing fake, by holding the ball properly in two hands and lifting it up as if taking a shot, by bending their knees and getting their head up (lifting their chin) so that more parts of the body contribute to the fake, instead of hands only.
- Strong, quick, powerful dribbles before taking the lay-up (two dribbles maximum).

PROGRESSION:
- A semiactive defender can be added onto player 5 (a defender who will maintain a presence when 5 attempts to score – but will not obstruct them). It can develop as a 1 vs 1 game with the defender becoming active.
- Player 5 will perform the same move but now will make a change of direction first and then will catch the ball and shoot straight away instead of taking a lay-up (see Fig. 48).

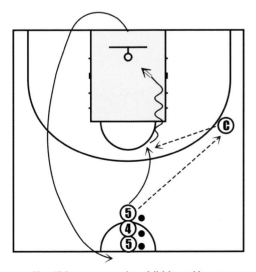

Fig. 47 Pass, cut, receive, dribble and lay-up shoot drill for centres.

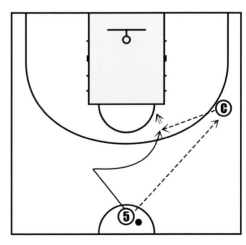

Fig. 48 Pass, cut, receive and jump shoot drill for centres.

PASS, POST UP, RECEIVE AND PLAY DRILL

Description: As in the previous drill, player 5 will pass the ball to the coach from the central circle and then will cut towards the basket. This time they will perform a cut from the middle of the free throw area to the low post on the same side where they passed the ball. Here they will post up with their back to the basket and receive the ball from the coach as seen in Fig. 49. Once in possession of the ball, player 5 will pivot so that they are facing the basket, will use one fake followed by one powerful dribble with the right hand and finish with a lay-up. Once player 5 finishes their move, player 4 will have their turn and so on.

Use/purpose: The drill is used to teach the centres to post up in the low post area (close to the basket). Apart from this, the ability to start with the back to the basket and then pivot and face the basket will be also developed. Lastly, it requires players to use (and/or learn/practise – depending on what stage of learning they are in) a range of moves suitable when playing centre position.

Materials and equipment required: One ball per player; one basket on a half court (with clear, visible marking on court).

Coaching points: Players need to be encouraged to:

- Send a good powerful pass to the coach.
- Use a good, convincing cut at the top of the key (before posting up).
- Get low once in low post when taking the post up position, by bending their knees and being well balanced.
- Get one arm up and 'ask for the ball'.

PROGRESSION:

- Use a fake before attacking the basket for a lay-up.
- When pivoting/turning to face the basket, take a jump shot instead of a lay-up.
- Add a semiactive defender who will put a bit of pressure on player 5 (for example during the cut or once in low post).
- Use various post moves when going to and finishing at the basket once they receive the ball, such as one dribble and spin move; hook shot or reverse lay-up.

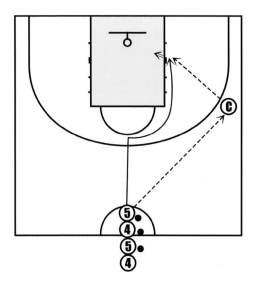

Fig. 49 Pass, post up, receive and play drill.

SPACING DRILL – CENTRE WITH GUARD WHO IS ON THE SAME SIDE OF THE COURT

Description: The initial set-up for the drill is with player 1 (guard) and player 5 (centre) positioned as in Fig. 50 (player 1 with a ball on the wing, level with free throw line, while 5 is on the low post, on the same side of the court). Player 1 will start by dribbling sideline–baseline on the way to the basket. As soon as 1 starts dribbling, player 5 will

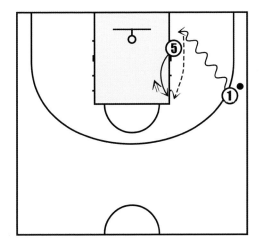

Fig. 50 Spacing drill – centre with guard who is on the same side of the court.

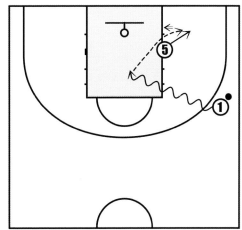

Fig. 51 Spacing drill – centre with guard who is on the same side of the court – with dribble drive towards the middle.

initiate a move towards the inside of the key, just below the elbow, creating space for 1 in this way. Player 5 will move sideways and backwards so that they keep their teammate and the ball in their eyesight all the time. Just before entering the key, 1 will pass the ball using a chest pass or bounce pass to 5, who will catch and shoot.

Use/purpose: This is a very good drill used to teach and apply the principles of spacing between a guard and a centre. The drill improves the playing relationship on court for the two players. Ability to read their colleague's game and action with the ball (when they do not have the ball) benefits too, alongside the ability to pass the ball. It can be used as a warm-up shooting drill from areas where the centre usually plays, but also in the later stages of a training session.

Materials and equipment required: One ball between two players; one basket on a half court.

Coaching points: Players need to be encouraged to:
- For player 5 – synchronize their move with their teammate: do not start too early or too late.

- For player 5 – do not have their back to the ball at any time during the drill. Make sure you see their teammates' moves all the time.
- For player 5 – have their hands out in front of them ready to catch the ball.
- For player 1 – keep their head up when dribbling.

PROGRESSION:
- Alternate the type of pass from 1 to 5 (such as chest pass, bounce pass or wrap around pass).
- After the catch, 5 can use one fake, one dribble and then shoot the ball.
- Add a passive defender on either player 1 or 5 (or on both).
- Repeat the same actions from the left-hand side of the court.
- Ask player 1 to drive towards the middle of the court on their way to the basket (instead of sideline–baseline) as in Fig. 51. This is when 5 will move towards the short corner area in order to create space for 1 and to receive the ball; after one-two dribbles, 1 will pass to 5 who will catch and shot.

SPACING DRILL BETWEEN GUARD AND CENTRE WHO IS ON OPPOSITE SIDE (ON THE WEAK SIDE)

Description: This drill is similar in nature to the previous one, the only difference being that, at the start, player 5 (centre) is on the low post in the weak side while 1 (guard) is on the opposite wing (*see* Fig. 52). Player 1 will dribble sideline–baseline on their way to the basket. After one or two dribbles, player 5 will start cutting towards the middle of the key in order to create space and to receive from 1 (they will have hands ready and will face the ball all the way). Player 5 will catch and shoot straight away.

Use/purpose: This is a very good drill to teach and apply the principles of spacing between a guard and a centre. The drill improves the playing relationship on court for the two players. The ability to read their colleague's game and action with the ball (when they do not have the ball) benefits too, alongside the ability to pass the ball. It can be used as a warm-up shooting drill from areas where the centre usually plays but also in the later stages of a training session.

Materials and equipment required: One ball between two players; one basket on a half court.

Coaching points: Players need to be encouraged to:
- For player 5 – synchronize their move with their teammates, not too early or late.
- For player 5 – to not have their back to the ball at any time during the drill. Make sure they can see their teammates' moves all the time.
- For player 5 – have their hands out in front of them ready to catch the ball.
- For player 1 – keep their head up when dribbling.

PROGRESSION:
- Alternate the type of pass from 1 to 5 (such as chest pass, bounce pass or wrap around pass).
- After the catch, player 5 can use one fake, one dribble and then shoot the ball.
- Add a passive defender on either player 1 or 5 (or on both).
- Repeat the same actions from the left-hand side of the court.
- Ask player 1 to drive towards the middle of the court on their way to the basket (instead of sideline-baseline) as in Fig. 53.

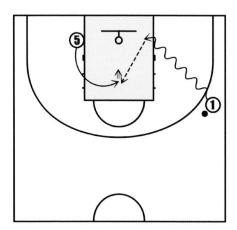

Fig. 52 Spacing drill between guard and centre who is on the opposite side (on the weak side).

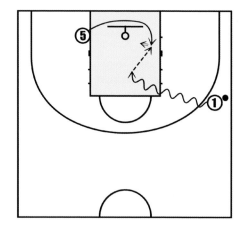

Fig. 53 Spacing drill between guard and centre who is on the opposite side (on the weak side) and dribble drive towards the middle of court.

This is when player 5 will move towards the opposite side of the key, going under the basket towards the new spot where they will catch and shoot.

COMBINATION OF CENTRE MOVES (SET A SCREEN, ROLL, RECEIVE, FINISH AT THE BASKET) DRILL

Description: All centres are in a queue at the top of the 3 points semicircle. One at a time, they will start by passing the ball to the coach (or to a passing player); after the pass they will go and set a screen on the cone or chair on the opposite side, just on the line that indicates the side of the three seconds space, as in Fig. 54. After setting the screen, the centre will roll towards the basket (their left shoulder will roll towards the middle of the court until they arrive under the basket) and this is when they will receive the ball from the coach and will finish at the basket using a variety of ways/moves: start for example with a semihook shot, a hook shot, a jump shot or a drop step.

Use/purpose: The drill is used to learn and practise moves and different ways to finish around the basket, which a centre would use. Ability to pass and go and set a screen away is also worked on, alongside the ability to set a screen and roll afterwards.

Materials and equipment required: One ball per player; one half court with one basket and clear court markings.

Coaching points: Players need to be encouraged to:
- Have their arms out when they roll after setting the screen – signal to their teammate that they are ready to receive the pass.
- Send a good powerful pass to the coach (or passing player).
- Make a strong cut towards the place where they will set a screen. When a player sets a screen, they should have their feet shoulder-width apart, arms in front of their chest but close to the body and stay in an upright position until they start to roll.

- Concentrate and try to score from the first attempt; in case they miss they should then get the rebound and put it back!

PROGRESSION:
- Use a fake as if they are shooting with the right hand, then pivot with the right foot, go under the basket and finish with the left hand (use an up and under move).
- Add another element into the drill after the centre receives the ball under the basket – for example one quick, powerful dribble with the right hand followed by a spin move and finish with left hand.
- Have a semiactive defender instead of the cone.
- Do the same drill from the opposite side – so now they will finish with the left hand (left-hand shooting).

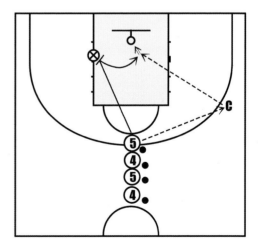

Fig. 54 Combination of centre moves (set a screen, roll, receive, finish at the basket) drill.

PART 2

DRILLS FOR SPECIFIC ACTIONS AND TECHNIQUES FOR OFFENCE AND FOR DEFENCE

5 DRILLS FOR PASSING

Offence is the most exciting part of the game – all players, irrespective of age and ability, want to shoot the ball and score! In addition, lots of people want to shoot from the distance (the 3 points shot) and all this excitement needs to be gradually incorporated into training sessions and the fun element to be maintained. Some of the great qualities that coaches will look for in their players when playing in offence include the capacity to score and also being unselfish – the ability to share the ball and to send an assist is to be appreciated and rewarded each time it happens. Lots of mistakes will happen in the beginning stages of learning and playing the game, mainly around the passing, dribbling and shooting (even professional players miss lots of shots) – this is when the coach's role comes into the equation, in the sense that they need to work with the players to build their confidence in scoring, sending a pass or dribbling without the fear of making a mistake.

Spacing, timing, ball movement and player movement are some of the modern concepts that are part of the game that impact significantly in the quality of any offence. This sub-chapter will incorporate drills for passing and catching the ball; shooting; dribbling; getting open; pivoting; offensive rebounding; setting a screen and screening. As all these techniques can be performed by any player on the team, the description of the drill and the use of it will contain an indication whether the drill is primarily for guards, for forwards or for centres.

PASSING IN THREE PLAYERS ON HALF OF A HALF COURT DRILL

Description: Players are divided into groups of three and each group will have one ball. They are placed on the court with player 1 holding the ball, player 2 on the wing and player 3 in the low post area so that they are all on one half of the half court, as illustrated in Fig. 55. The drill requires players to pass the ball and move as soon as they have made a pass or even before the pass comes to them, in order to get open – in this way they will set a screen for the open man (player without the ball), exchange positions between them, cut towards the basket and so on. Start with four passes and at the end of the fourth pass, that

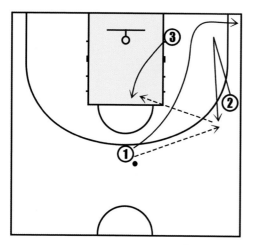

Fig. 55 Passing in three players on half of a half court drill.

player who now has the ball will be required to shoot the ball in order to score, as in Figs. 56 and 57. After a shot is made, all players need to go and get the rebound.

Use/purpose: The drill requires players to constantly pass and to move when they do not have the ball. It also encourages players to concentrate on what they have to do when they do not have the ball (playing without the ball) and also the number of passes they have up to that moment.

Materials and equipment required: One ball; one half of a court.

Coaching points: Players need to be encouraged to:

• Send strong passes to the open teammate.
• Have their arms out in front of their shoulders, ready to catch the ball.
• Cut powerfully to a new spot on the court – try to sprint instead of jogging!

PROGRESSION:

• Start with four passes and then ask players for six passes and shoot, seven passes and shoot and so on.
• Ask for four passes and indicate that player 3 should shoot the ball on the fourth pass (make sure you number the players from 1 to 3 at the start of the drill).
• Ask for six passes and player 2 to shoot the ball.
• Ask for eight passes and player 1 to shoot the ball.
• Ask for ten passes and this time the coach will announce who shoots the ball after the fifth pass is made.

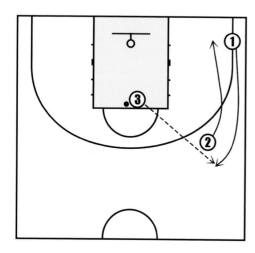

Fig. 56 Passing in three players on half of a half court drill (continuation).

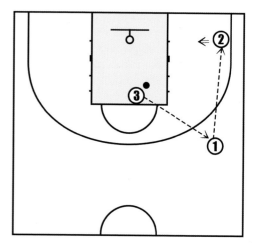

Fig. 57 Passing in three players on half of a half court drill – shot after fourth pass.

FOUR CORNERS PASSING DRILL

Description: The group of players is divided into four queues (minimum eight players needed), with one queue at each corner of a half court (*see* Fig. 58). Player 1 has one ball and will pass to player 4 using a chest pass; and then player 1 cuts inside the court and receives the pass back from player 4. Player 1 will pass now to player 7 and then 1 joins the end of the queue where they passed to (behind 16). After passing to player 1, 4 will cut inside, towards the middle of court. Player 7 who now has the ball will pass to player 4 and then 4 will pass to 10 (and then 4 will join the back of the queue behind player 13). Player 10 will pass to player 7, then 7 will pass to 2 and 7 joins the back of the queue behind 14. And the drill continues following the same pattern.

Use/purpose: The drill is used to practise passing skills (sending and receiving/catching the ball). Apart from this, cutting into space after making a pass is being practised too.

Materials and equipment required: One ball; one half of a court.

Coaching points: Players need to be encouraged to:

- Send accurate passes – leave their arms extended after the pass.
- Pass and cut – when they cut, have their arms out (show their hands) and be ready to catch the ball.
- Always catch the ball with both hands.

PROGRESSION:

- Alternate the type of pass that is required – such as bounce pass; one-hand pass.
- A second ball could be introduced.

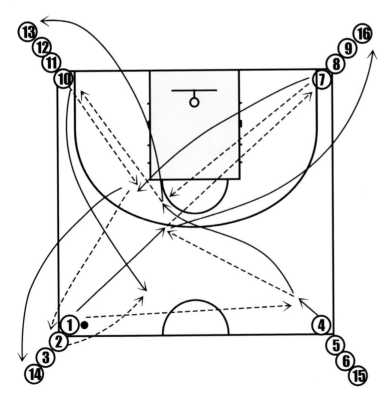

Fig. 58 Four corners passing drill.

DRILL FOR PASSING – LONG PASSES ON FULL COURT DRILL

Description: Players 1 and 6 have a ball each and they start the drill from under the basket; all other players are grouped in two queues, with each queue close to the sideline of the court, as seen in Fig. 59. The drill starts with 1 and 6 who will pass at the same time to players 5 and 7 (1 will pass to 5 while 6 will pass to 7). After they catch the ball, players 5 and 7 will dribble towards the basket and they are followed by players 4 and 8 respectively – players 4 and 8 will chase 5 and 7, trying to stop them from scoring. After passing to 5, player 1 will join the queue to their right-hand side behind player 2 while player 6 will join the queue behind 10.

Players 5 and 7 will take a lay-up first and afterwards they move to the back of the opposite queue (5 will end up behind 6 and 7 behind 1). Players 4 and 8 will rebound and they will pass the ball to 9 and to 3 (4 will pass to 9 while 8 will pass to 3). Player 9 will be chased/followed by 10, while player 3 will be

chased by 2 and the drill continues following the same pattern.

Use/purpose: The drill develops the ability to send a long pass. It encourages players to rebound and immediately to send a long pass (a fastbreak type of pass). The ability to see the floor and to finish under pressure are also practised.

Materials and equipment required: Two basketballs; one full court with two baskets and full court markings. A minimum of ten players is needed.

Coaching points: Players need to be encouraged to:

- Send a strong, powerful pass all the way to the other side of court (over the halfway line).
- Go and get the rebound while the ball is in the air in case of a missed shot (or directly from the net if basket is scored).
- Try and communicate (or signal with their hand up) to their teammate that they are ready to receive the ball.

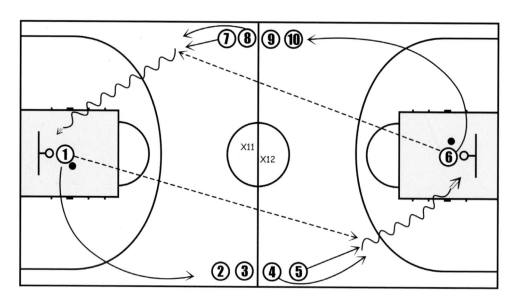

Fig. 59 Drill for passing – long passes on full court drill.

PROGRESSION:
- Add two defenders (X11 and X12) in the central circle – their role is to intercept the passes that are not that strong.
- Take a jump shot instead of a lay-up.
- A time limit can be added – such as thirty seconds or one minute – and see how many points they score.

- In order to make it easier (for example with beginners and with young players who do not have enough power in their arms to send such a long pass) – players can add one to two dribbles maximum before sending the pass to their team-mates (dribbling action towards the free throw line on the court they are on).

DRILL FOR PASSING – OUTLET PASS DRILL

Description: Four players are positioned in front of one basket as in Fig. 60: players 1 and 2 are on the 3 points line while players 3 and 4 are inside the key, close to the basket. Players 1 and 2 are shooting players while players 3 and 4 will rebound and send an outlet pass every time they rebound when a shot is taken. Player 2 has the ball and will start the drill by taking the shot. Player 3 will rebound and will send an outlet pass to 2 who will cut to the opposite wing after their shot (*see* Fig. 60). If the basket is scored, 3 will get the ball and inbound it to player 2,(*see* Fig. 61).

As soon as they receive from 3, 2 will pass the ball to 1 and then 2 will cut across the court back at the starting spot (*see* Fig. 62). On receiving the pass from 2, 1 will take the shot, which will be rebounded by 4. After the

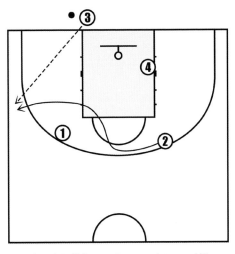

Fig. 61 Drill for passing – outlet pass drill (continuation).

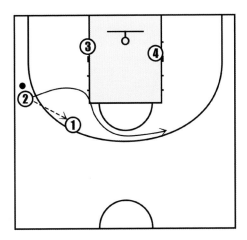

Fig. 62 Drill for passing – outlet pass drill (continuation).

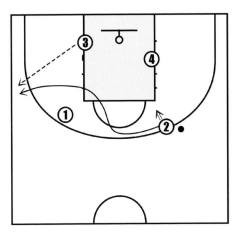

Fig. 60 Drill for passing – outlet pass drill.

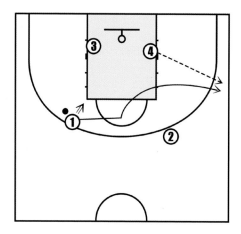

Fig. 63 Drill for passing – outlet pass drill (continuation with player 4 sending an outlet pass to 1).

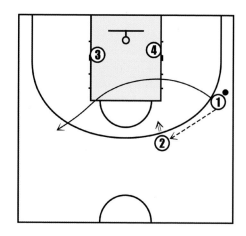

Fig. 64 Drill for passing – outlet pass drill (continuation – with player 2 shooting).

rebound, 4 will send an outlet pass to 1; after taking the shot, 1 will cut across the court on the wing spot (see Fig. 63). As soon as they receive the ball from 4, 1 will pass to 2 who will shoot and the drill continues following the same pattern (*see* Fig. 64). After a number of shots, switch roles between players 1 and 2 with 3 and 4 (so now 3 and 4 become shooters and 1 and 2 become rebounders).

Use/purpose: The drill allows players to learn and practise how to send an outlet pass. Shooting and rebounding actions are being worked on; cutting and getting into the ideal position on the wing to receive the outlet pass is another aim of the drill.

Materials and equipment required: One ball on a half court with one basket. Four players needed (minimum).

Coaching points: Players need to be encouraged to:

- Catch the ball with arms fully extended when getting the rebound, while the ball is in the air. After the catch, keep the ball

level with their chest (or above) so that a good, quick pass can then be made (easily and quickly).

- Send a signal to their teammate who got the rebound so that they know where to send the outlet pass (either say 'outlet' or have one arm up or both).

- Make sure the exercise flows, with players not having any breaks between their actions! You can set up a time limit perhaps or a specific number of shots made.

PROGRESSION:

- Players 3 and 4 can compete against each other (playing 1 vs 1) in order to get the rebound – and who gets the rebound then will send the outlet pass.

- A semiactive defender can be introduced to guard player 1 or 2. The defender needs to maintain a presence and not necessarily to obstruct the attackers (do not block their shots, do not intercept the ball, and so on).

PASSING IN THREES ON FULL COURT DRILL

Description: Groups of three players, with one ball per group. All three players start

running forward at the same time – player 2 has the ball and will pass to 1 who cuts/runs forward. Once the ball is received, player 1 will send a long pass across the court to player 3 on the other side of the court; player 3 will catch, dribble once or twice maximum and will take the lay-up, as in Fig. 65.

Use/purpose: The drill is used to practise and improve passing while running (and the ability to catch and pass while on the move towards the opposite basket).

Materials and equipment required: One ball per group of three players; one full court.

Coaching points: Players need to be encouraged to:

- Send good, powerful, accurate passes so that the receiving player runs into the path of the pass.

- Keep running forward if they do not have the ball.
- Always catch the ball with both hands.

PROGRESSION:

- Same pattern as before but this time player 3 will catch the ball and wait (while dribbling stationary) for player 2 to arrive – player 2 will run forward and will make a change of direction to cut towards the basket in order to catch from player 3 and take a lay-up (*see* Fig. 66).
- Ask for four passes and a lay-up: players 2 and 1 will exchange three passes while player 3 runs on the opposite side. Player 1 will send the fourth pass to 3 who will catch and will take a lay-up (*see* Fig. 67).

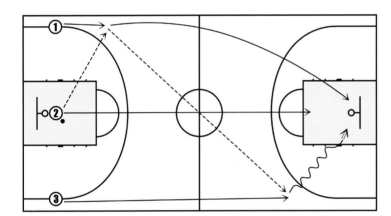

Fig. 65 Passing in 3s on full court drill.

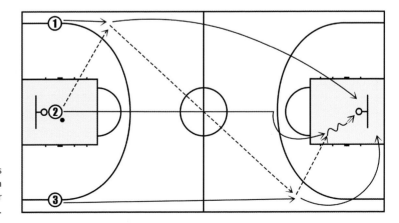

Fig. 66 Passing in 3s on full court drill with player 2 shooting after change of direction.

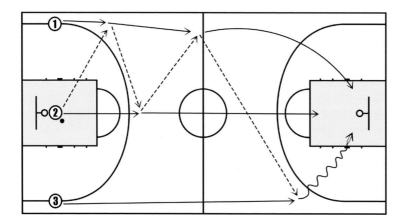

Fig. 67 Passing in 3s on full court drill with player 3 shooting.

3 vs 2 PASSING WHILE DRIBBLING/FROM DRIBBLING DRILL

Description: Five players at the time are within a cone-restricted area as in Fig. 68, with players 1, 2 and 3 as attackers while 4 and 5 start as defenders. The purpose of the drill is to play a passing game following 'pig in the middle' principles only in the area determined by the cones – attackers are required to dribble two to three times maximum and then to pass the ball (so continuous dribbling and passing). If players 4 or 5 intercept (or touch) the ball, they switch roles – they replace the attackers.

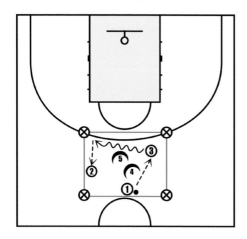

Fig. 68 3 vs 2 passing while dribbling/from dribbling drill.

Use/purpose: The drill is used in order to practise dribbling while under pressure from the defender. Passing ability under pressure and in a limited space is also being developed.

Materials and equipment required: One ball and four cones on a flat surface.

Coaching points: Players need to be encouraged to:

- Keep their head up when dribbling.
- Protect the ball with the non-dribbling hand and foot – for a right-hand dribble use left arm and left foot to protect the ball (*see* Fig. 69).
- Use fakes (passing fakes).
- When receiving the ball make sure they catch it with both hands.
- For attackers – move into space and try to get open so that they receive the ball.

PROGRESSION:

- When passing the ball, attackers are not allowed to actually catch the ball with both hands and pass it. The pass must be sent off the dribble with one hand only; if they catch with both hands (so if they have both hands on the ball) and pass, then they become a defender.

Fig. 69 Player who is protecting the ball with their body.

FASTBREAK INITIATED WITH PASS FROM THE CORNER DRILL

Description: Groups of three players with one ball between three for the top two groups in the queue. Player 3 has the ball and starts the drill by passing to player 1 who immediately will pass to 2. Player 2 will return the pass to 1 who now will take one to two dribbles maximum towards the opposite basket, and then will pass diagonally to player 3 who is sprinting to take part on fastbreak on the right wing to receive and take a lay-up (*see* Fig. 70). After passing to player 3, player 1 will go right towards the sideline of the court in order to receive from player 2 who will collect the rebound from the shot taken by 3 (*see* Fig. 71).

Player 1 will pass to player 9 – this will happen somewhere just outside the court so that these three returning players do not obstruct the next group of three players (4, 5 and 6) who will have their turn. A target could be set, for example to score fifteen to twenty times in ninety seconds (or twenty to twenty-five makes in two minutes and so on); this will depend on the ability of the team and the first time this drill is performed the score can be used as a benchmark for the future.

Use/purpose: This exercise is very useful to work and improve the fastbreak and quick offence principles. Passing while running and sprinting towards the opposite basket are being practised too. The drill could be also used as a conditioning drill in the main part of a session, primarily in the pre-season and during the season.

Materials and equipment required: Two balls; one full court with two hoops and clear court markings.

Coaching points: Players need to be encouraged to:

- Send a strong, accurate pass.
- Sprint forward when they do not have the ball and be ahead of the ball.
- Concentrate in order to score the lay-up every time it's their turn.

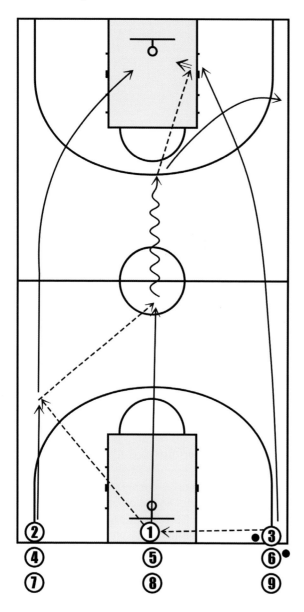

Fig. 70 Fastbreak initiated with pass from the corner drill.

- Rebound the ball preferably before it touches the floor.
- Jog back to the end of the queue (instead of walking).

PROGRESSION:
- With more advanced players you can increase the time to two and a half or three minutes.
- You can add a rule that requires the group who misses a lay-up to run one more length after the drill is over (one extra length for every missed lay-up).

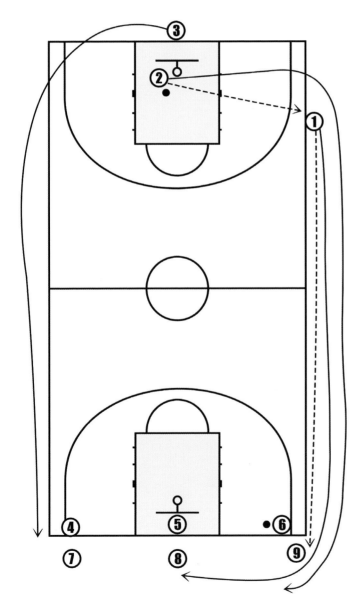

Fig. 71 Fastbreak initiated with pass from the corner drill – with player 3 shooting and 2 rebounding.

6 DRILLS FOR SHOOTING

SHOOTING FROM THE WING AND FROM THE CORNER DRILL

Description: The group of players is divided into two groups (queues) who are situated in the middle of the court with players 2 and 4 on the wing, level with free throw line extended (*see* Fig. 72). The drill starts with player 1 passing to player 2 and player 3 passing to player 4 (at the same time). Once they receive the ball, players 2 and 4 will catch and shoot straight away. The drill then continues with player 1 who will go/cut to the wing and receive from player 5 – at the same time player 3 will do the same on the other side (3 will receive from 7) – then catch and shoot as shown in Fig. 73. After taking their shot, 2 and 4 will rebound their

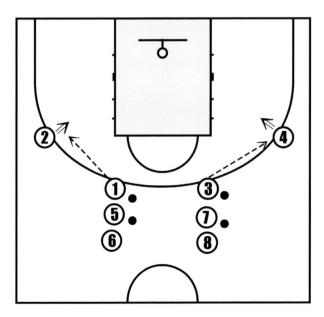

Fig. 72 Shooting from the wing and from the corner drill.

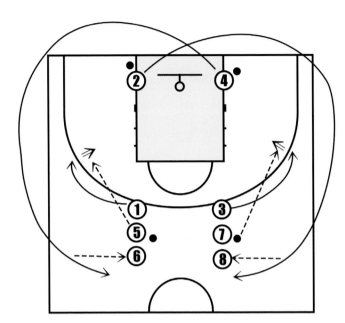

Fig. 73 Shooting from the wing and from the corner drill (continuation – with players 1 and 3 shooting).

own shot and will join the back of the opposite queue. And the drill continues following the same pattern (cut to the wing, receive, shoot, and so on).

Use/purpose: The purpose of the drill is to get players used to the idea of getting open and catching and shooting straight away. Passing is being practised too. The drill can be used as a warm-up activity and also as a component part of the later stages in the session.

Materials and equipment required: Four basketballs; one basket. Minimum six to eight players on one half court.

Coaching points: Players need to be encouraged to:

- Be well balanced when taking the shot, using the power generated by the legs and making sure they follow through.
- Send a good, well-timed, accurate pass to their teammate.
- Have their arms ready when cutting so that they show a target to their teammate when they pass.

PROGRESSION:

- On the catch – use one fake, one quick dribble and catch and shoot.
- Players 1 and 3 will dribble towards the elbow (free throw line) and will pass to players 2 and 4 respectively, towards the corner of the court. Players 2 and 4 will

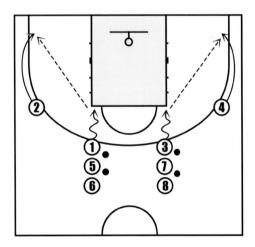

Fig. 74 Shooting from the wing and from the corner drill (continuation – with players 1 and 3 dribbling and passing to the corners).

initiate their cut towards the corner of the court as soon as 1 and 3 start dribbling the ball (*see* Fig. 74). Players 2 and 4 will catch and shoot, rebound their own shot and continue the drill as before.

- Players 1 and 3 will pass to players 2 and to 4 respectively on the wing and then will go and set a screen to the player they passed to. Players 2 and 4 will use the screen and will start dribbling the ball towards the basket in order to take a lay-up or a jump shot (see Fig. 75).
- Use a dribble-hand off action instead of pass and screen.

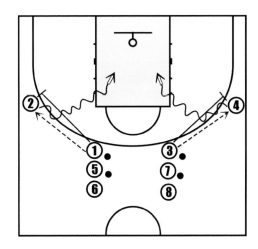

Fig. 75 Shooting from the wing and from the corner drill (continuation – with players 1 and 3 passing and setting a screen on the ball).

SHOOTING DRILL FROM THREE QUEUES SET UP

Description: Players are grouped in three queues as follows: players 1, 2 and 3 on the corner (with a ball each); players 4, 5 and 6 on the halfway line right next to the side line (inside the court) while 7, 8 and 9 are in the central circle (see Fig. 76). Player 1 starts the drill by passing the ball to player 4 and then 1 will cut to the elbow on the same side of

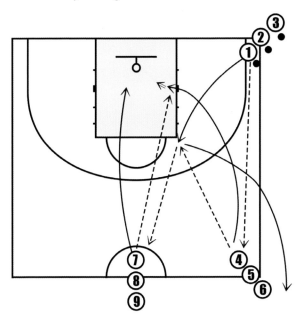

Fig. 76 Shooting drill from three queues set-up.

court (flash high to the elbow). Player 4 will return the pass to player 1 and then 4 will cut to the basket in order to receive from 7 (who, meanwhile, receives the pass from 1). After the pass to 7, 1 will go behind 6 after passing to 4, player 7 will go and get the rebound and then will join the queue behind 3. After taking the lay-up shot, player 4 will jog and join the queue behind 9, so all players will rotate clockwise (see Fig. 77). The drill continues with player 2 passing to 5 and so on.

Use/purpose: The drill can be used as a warm-up activity with all players (irrespective of the position they play) in order to practise passing, moving and cutting to the basket without the ball, and rebounding. It also improves communication. It can be used as a competitive drill by having two teams (one team at each basket) and deciding on a specific number of points to be scored or allocating a time limit (such as one to two minutes).

Materials and equipment required: Three balls; one basket on a half court. Minimum nine players or more.

Coaching points: Players need to be encouraged to:

- Send a powerful, accurate pass to teammates.
- Cut powerfully to the basket and have arms out, ready to catch the ball.
- To improve communication make sure they call the name of the person they are

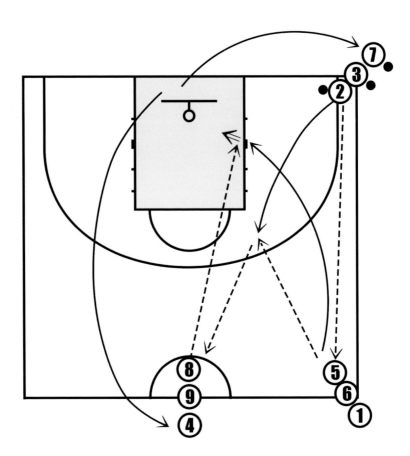

Fig. 77 Shooting drill from three queues set-up (continuation).

going to pass to and also count with a loud voice each time a basket is scored.

- Try to get the rebound before the ball touches the ground, while it is in the air.

PROGRESSION:

- Instead of taking a lay-up, ask players to take a jump shot (receive just outside the key, catch and shoot).
- Ask players to catch the ball, use a fake (such as a shooting fake or driving fake) and then one powerful dribble (diagonally either towards the right or the left) and shoot from the dribble (shoot off the dribble).

- With teams that are more advanced, ask them to count and aim for fifteen or twenty makes as a team. If they miss four or five consecutive shots during this attempt, then they will go back to zero.
- Do the same from the left-hand side – the queues will be positioned as in Fig. 78 and the players will rotate anticlockwise.

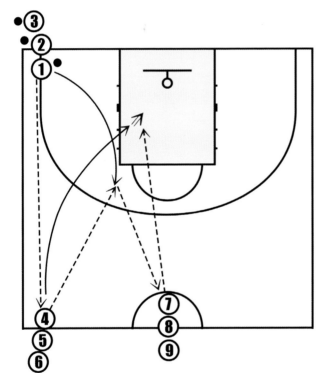

Fig. 78 Shooting drill from three queues set-up – continuation from left-hand side.

ELBOW SHOOTING FOR CENTRES DRILL

Description: Player 5 (centre) has a ball and is positioned in the short corner (*see* Fig. 79). They will pass the ball to passing player P and then they will make a quick fake (one to two steps towards the basket) after which they will flash high to the elbow on the same side of the court. They will receive from the passing player, will pivot towards the basket (square to the basket) and take the jump shot (using a catch and shoot action). After the shot,

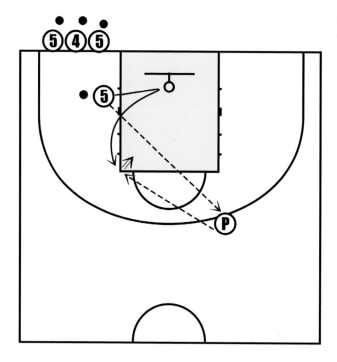

Fig. 79 Elbow shooting for centres drill.

player 5 will collect their own rebound and join the back of the queue and another player steps on court to have their go.

Use/purpose: This drill can be used as part of the individualization process for centres. The purposes include to practise the skip pass; getting open in an area where they are usually active during the game (elbow area); and to practise shooting when facing the basket (catch and shoot).

Materials and equipment required: One ball per player; one basket on a half court and one passing player.

Coaching points: Players need to be encouraged to:

- Send a powerful, accurate pass (skip pass) to the passing player.

- Execute a convincing change of direction before getting open at the elbow area.
- Catch the ball with both hands and square to the basket.
- Take a good, well-balanced shot and leave their arm extended after the shot (follow through).

PROGRESSION:

- A semiactive defender can be introduced to guard the centre.
- Two consecutive actions (or more) can be incorporated – alternating the starting position from right to left; adding a fake after the catch and so on.

DRILL FOR SHOOTING FROM SHORT CORNER AREA (FOR CENTRES)

Description: From the low post area, player 5 (centre) will pass the ball to passing player P who is at the top of the 3 points semicircle, slightly towards the wing area (*see* Fig. 80). After sending

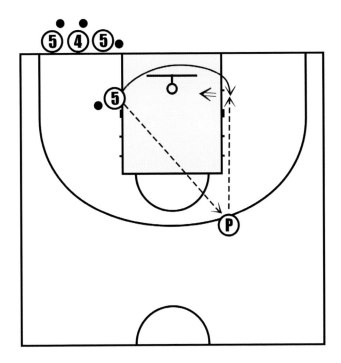

Fig. 80 Drill for shooting from short corner area (for centres).

the pass, player 5 will cut across the lane (by going close to the baseline, under the basket) to the opposite short corner where they will receive the pass, will pivot towards the basket (square up to the basket) and will take the shot (catch and shoot). They then collect their own rebound and join the back of the queue outside the court so that the next player can have a go.

Use/purpose: The drill is primarily used in order to get the centres to practise sending a skip pass, to get open in the short corner area (from one side of the paint to the other), and to practise shooting (catch and shoot) after using a pivoting move.

Materials and equipment required: One ball per player; one basket on one half court and one passing player.

Coaching points: Players need to be encouraged to:

- Send an accurate, powerful skip pass to the passing player.

- Cut powerfully to the opposite short corner area and have their arms out, ready to catch and shoot.
- Square up to the basket so that they end up in a well-balanced position, facing the basket.
- Take the shot from a balanced position, with feet shoulder-width apart and follow through once the ball is released.

PROGRESSION:
- A semiactive defender can be introduced to guard the centre.
- Two consecutive actions (or more) can be incorporated – alternating the starting position from right to left; adding a fake after the catch and so on.
- On the catch – ask the centre to play 1 vs 1 against the defender guarding them (so the defender becomes active).

ELBOW AND SHORT CORNER SHOOTING DRILL FOR CENTRES

Description: Player 4 who is in the low post will pass the ball to player 5, who will cut from the right elbow to the left elbow (*see* Fig. 81). Player 5 will catch and shoot, collect their own rebound and move to the opposite queue. After passing to player 5, player 4 will cut on the baseline to the short corner area where they will receive from player 3 – player 4 will square to the basket and take the shot, then rebound their own shot and join the opposite queue. The drill continues with player 2 passing the ball to player 3, who is cutting to the left elbow and will catch and shoot; after passing to player 3, player 2 will cut baseline to the opposite short corner and receives from player 6 to catch and shoot and so on.

Use/purpose: This is a useful drill for centres who will need to shoot the ball from the areas of the court where they usually play; cut and get open to elbow and short corner; perform a catch and shoot action. It can be used as a warm-up drill at one basket or even as a competitive drill with two teams of six players (one group at each basket) to practise shooting actions.

Materials and equipment required: Five basketballs for six players; one basket on one half court; two cones (or chairs).

Coaching points: Players need to be encouraged to:

*   Send an accurate, powerful chest pass to the passing player.
*   Cut powerfully to the opposite short corner area and have their arms out, ready to catch and shoot.
*   Square up to the basket and pivot so that they end up in a well-balanced position, facing the basket.
*   Take the shot from a balanced position, with feet shoulder-width apart and follow through once the ball is released.

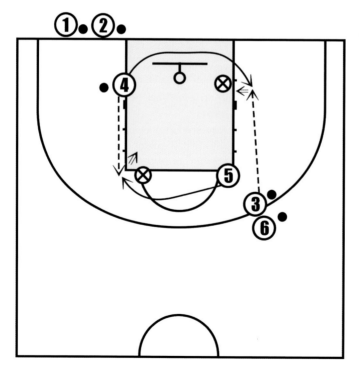

Fig. 81 Elbow and short corner shooting drill for centres.

PROGRESSION:
- Change the type of pass – for example a bounce pass instead of chest pass. Also, ask players to keep dribbling the ball and send a one-hand pass to their teammates.
- Make a fake before the players start to cut and to move to the position where they shoot from.

- Count the number of made shots. You can set a target to score for example ten or fifteen as a whole group.
- Same as above but now tell players that if they miss three or four shots in a row the whole group goes back to zero, and restart counting on the way to the initial target (such as ten or fifteen).
- Change the position of cones and where to cut in order to shoot (*see* Fig. 82).

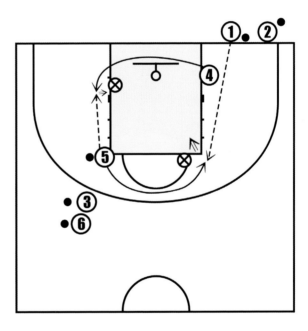

Fig. 82 Elbow and short corner shooting drill for centres (continuation with a new set-up for the spots to take the shots from).

ALL THREE PLAYERS SHOOT DRILL
(THREE PLAYERS AND FIVE BALLS DRILL)

Description: All players in the team are divided into groups of three players (the distribution of players can be one guard, one forward and one centre) as follows: players 1, 2 and 3 start the drill from one end of the court; players 4, 5 and 6 are just outside the court at the opposite end with players 4 and 6 having a ball each, on the corner of the court, while player 5 is positioned under the basket area; players 7, 8 and 9 are positioned similarly to players 4, 5 and 6 in the sense that players 7 and 8 have a ball each and are at the corners of the court while player 8 is under the basket. Players 1, 2 and 3 start the drill with 1 passing to 2, 2 passing to 3 and 3 passing to 1 following the 3 men weave drill principles (*see* Fig. 83). After these three passes, player 1 arrives at the free throw line level where they will go and take a lay-up. At the same time, player 2 will go wide, close to the side-line, and will receive the pass from player 6 and will take a jump shot. Similarly, player 3 will do the same on the opposite side – receive from 4 and take a jump shot. Players 2 and 3 will rebound their own shots and replace players 4 and 6 who will now go towards the opposite basket together with player 5 (who has rebounded the shot from 1) following the same three-man weave principles with three passes and all three players taking a shot at the opposite end (*see* Fig. 84).

Use/purpose: While the drill is primarily a shooting drill (so shooting as a skill is being worked on), it also enhances the ability to pass to teammates and move/cut on the court without the ball. Catch and shoot is encouraged as well as going to collect their own rebound. It

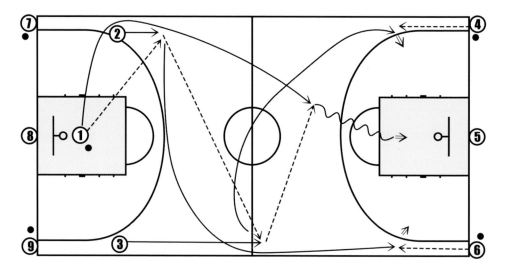

Fig. 83 All three players shoot drill (three players and five balls drill).

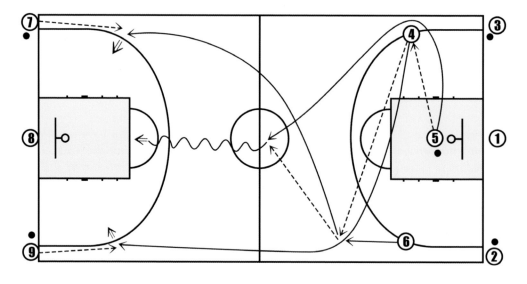

Fig. 84 All three players shoot drill (three players and five balls drill) – with players 4, 5 and 6 shooting.

can be used as a part of the warming up and also of the main part of a training session (even as a conditioning drill).

Materials and equipment required: Five balls; one full court with two baskets. Nine players minimum.

Coaching points: Players need to be encouraged to:

- Sprint forward when they do not have the ball so that they are always ahead of the ball.
- Have their arms out in front of their chest ready to receive the pass.
- Try to get a well-balanced shot when they receive the pass from teammates who are in the corners. Leave the arm extended and follow through.

- Send a good, powerful, well-timed pass to teammates.

PROGRESSION:

- All three players take jump shots only – player 1 will stop at the free throw line and take a jump shot instead of a lay-up.
- Set a time limit (such as two minutes or three minutes) and count how many points are being scored by all nine players. Use this info as a standard/comparison for next time you run the drill.
- Each time they receive from the corner, catch the ball, use a fake and one quick dribble right or left and take the shot off the dribble.

SHOOTING DRILL FOR THREE PLAYERS WITH TWO BALLS (FULL COURT)

Description: Two basketballs for each group of three players. Player 1 is at the elbow and will receive a pass from player 2 (who is just outside the court) – player 1 will catch and shoot while player 2 will sprint towards the other end in order to receive a pass from 3 and do the same (catch and shoot) as shown in Fig. 85. After passing to 2, player 3 will sprint towards the other end in order to receive from 1 who by now has collected their own rebound (see Fig. 86). This group of three players will take shots from the elbow areas and at the same

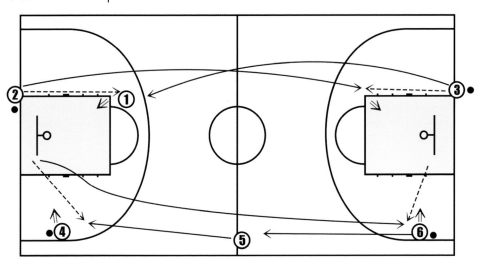

Fig. 85 Shooting drill for three players with two balls (full court).

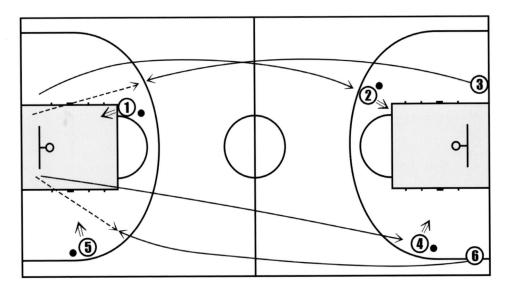

Fig. 86 Shooting drill for three players with two balls (full court) – with player 3 receiving from 1.

time another group of 3 players (4, 5 and 6) will be on court performing a similar action – they will shoot from the baseline at both ends of the court. A limit can be imposed – first player to score five times as an individual (or ten, fifteen times with more advanced players) wins.

Use/purpose: The drill is primarily designed to work on 'catch and shoot' after sprinting from one end to the other. It can be used as a warming-up activity; as a drill at a session when you have low number of players attending (six for example); even as a conditioning drill when you set up a time limit; or as a shooting competition between groups.

Materials and equipment required: One full court; two balls per group of three players.

Coaching points: Players need to be encouraged to:

- Send good, accurate passes.
- Sprint (instead of jog) and stop quickly in order to catch and shoot.
- Take a good shot, well-balanced, and follow through after the ball is released.
- They can dribble the ball a couple of times around the area where they got the rebound by the time their teammate arrives.

PROGRESSION:

- Take off the dribble shots (after the catch they make a quick fake, one dribble to the side right or left and shoot the ball).

SCORE TWO IN A ROW
(FROM TWELVE SPOTS ON THE COURT) DRILL

Description: Each player has a ball. The drill is performed individually, and the purpose of the drill is to score two jump shots in a row from every single spot (from every single cone) out of the twelve spots (cones) that are on the court. Player 1 will start on spot 1 (at the same time player 2 starts on spot 2, player 3 on spot 3 and so on) as shown in Fig. 87 and will take the first shot: if they make it, they will attempt their second shot from the

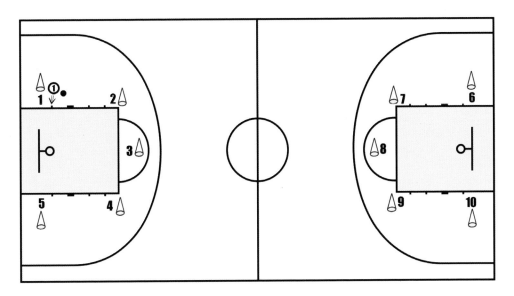

Fig. 87 Score two in a row (from twelve spots on the court) drill.

same spot after getting their own rebound; if they miss it, they will have to sprint (while dribbling) towards the other end of court and go to spot 6 for example, where they will attempt to score two shots in a row. If they make two in a row at spot 1 they will then go to spot 2 and so on, following the same principle – they have to run towards the other basket each time they miss one shot (if they make two in a row from spot 6 then they go to spot 7).

Use/purpose: This is a drill that requires a high number of jump shots from all the players, irrespective of the position that they play (practising shooting skills) and also full concentration and focus in order to score two in a row. Dribbling while running is also practised. This is a very competitive drill, which could be used in any part of the training session and at any time during the season.

Materials and equipment required: One ball per player; a full court with clear markings and two baskets; twelve markers on court (or twelve cones).

Coaching points: Players need to be encouraged to:

- Take a good shot every single time – well-balanced (with feet shoulder width apart preferably, knees flexed), facing the basket and follow through by leaving the arm extended after the shot.
- Give enough height to the ball (the ball should travel in an inverted U shape) and also flick their wrist powerfully so that they give rotation/spin to the ball.
- Keep their head up when dribbling towards the opposite basket.

PROGRESSION:

- Depending on the ability of your players you can have less spots with beginners (six or eight instead of twelve) and also spots that are close to the basket. You can increase the distance (from the spot to the basket) with more advanced players.
- Set a time limit that players have available to complete this drill.
- With more advanced players, the first shot could be a 2 points shot and the second shot could be a 3 points shot!

'33 POINTS' SHOOTING DRILL (COMPETITION)

Description: The group of players is divided into two teams with an equal number of players. The first player in each team will start shooting at the same time when a signal is given (*see* Fig. 88) and the main purpose of the drill is to score exactly 33 points while respecting certain strict rules: the two teams need to start with a made 3 points shot and finish exactly on 33 with another 3 points made shot! With the exception of the first shot and the last shot (which both need to be a 3 points shot), players have a choice of 1, 2 or 3 points – when it's their turn, a player can chose to take a lay-up that is worth 1 point, a jump shot from outside the key that is 2 points or a 3 points shot from behind the 3 points semicircle. Every time a player scores, the whole team needs to count with a loud voice and add the respective points to their overall score. When it's their turn, each player has one shot only and they need to get their own rebound after taking the shot (made or miss), pass to the next player and join the back of the queue. The drill requires focus and lots of attention, especially with regards to keeping the score because this will determine what type of shot needs to be taken (a 1 point, 2 points or 3 points shot). For example, if a team gets to 29 points the next player needs to take a lay-up worth 1 point (which makes the total 30) followed by the next player with a 3 points shot so that the team finishes exactly on 33 points and wins the game. If they take a 2 points shot when they get to 29, this will give them 29+2=31, and with a 3 points made shot they cannot finish exactly on 33 (31+3=34), so they lose the game!

Use/purpose: A very competitive and fun drill that requires attention, concentration, decision-making and quick thinking with regards to the type of shot that needs to be taken from all players involved. Players will take a high number of shots so shooting skills are being practised. It can be used in any part of the training session and also at any moment during the season.

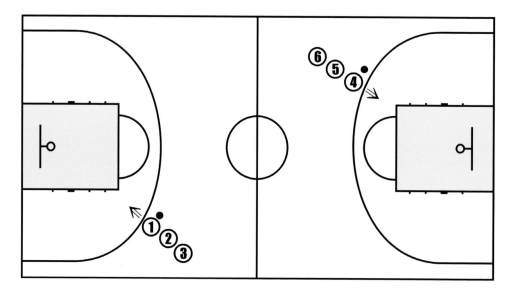

Fig. 88 '33 points' shooting drill (competition).

Materials and equipment required: One ball per team; one full court with two baskets and full court markings.

Coaching points: Players need to be encouraged to:

- Take a good shot every time – well balanced, with elbow under the ball, follow through and so on.
- Go and rebound their own shot quickly and send an accurate pass to their team-mate who is next in the queue.

- Have their arms out in front of the chest, ready to catch and shoot, every time they are at the front of the queue.

PROGRESSION:

- Choose different spots on the court to take the shots from (such as top, 45-degree angle, baseline).
- With more advanced players – the drill can be performed by taking only 3 point shots.

FIVE MINUTES – FOUR SPOTS SHOOTING DRILL

Description: The drill is being performed by all players in the team/squad (eight to ten or more) as part of the same group. There are four spots on the court where players will shoot from: in turn, they keep shooting for ninety seconds from the first spot, then for another ninety seconds from the second spot and so on from the third and fourth spot for a total of five minutes. In order to do so, players are divided into a shooting queue and a passing queue. Player 1, who has a ball and is at the front of the shooting queue, will take the first shot, will rebound their own shot and then will pass to player 6, who is the first without a ball in the passing queue and then joins the back of the queue behind player 8 (see Fig. 89 and Fig. 90). Immediately after player 1 takes the shot, player 2 will continue to do the same after receiving the pass from player 5 and in this way, one at a time, taking turns,

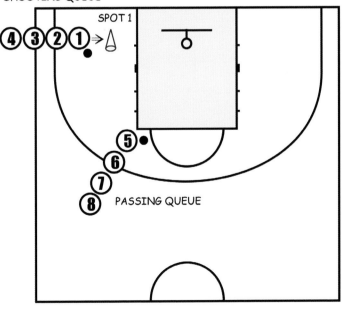

Fig. 89 Five minutes – four spots shooting drill.

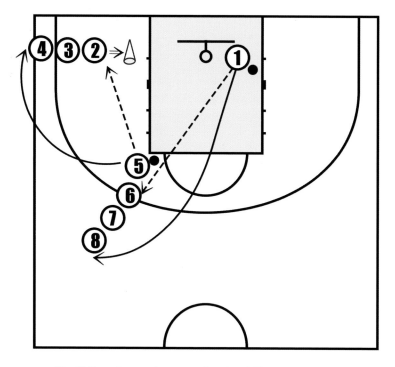

Fig. 90 Five minutes – four spots shooting drill (continuation).

all players will be shooting (and rebounding) and all players will be passing. After the first ninety seconds, the players will start shooting from the second spot and this is when the passing queue will become the shooting queue and the other way round (*see* Fig. 91 and Fig. 92). The drill continues for the next ninety seconds following the same principles (shoot, get own rebound, pass the ball to the passing queue and join the back of it) and afterwards the players will move one spot towards the right side of the court (*see* Fig. 93 and Fig. 94). After another ninety seconds, the players will move the queue one last time so that they shoot from the fourth spot and pass from where spot three was (*see* Figs. 95 and 96). Every time a shot is made this is worth 1 point. At the end of the five minutes (four spots × ninety seconds = five minutes), the players need to indicate to their coach the total number of points scored (they need to keep counting with a loud voice every

time a basket is scored for the whole duration of the five minutes). The total should be around a minimum of 60–70 points with senior teams and players that play at a decent level and even higher (80–90 or more) with more advanced teams. The first time a team runs this drill, the final score can then act as a benchmark – as a record for the team that needs to be improved next time the team runs the drill again.

Use/purpose: This is a shooting drill designed to practise jump shots. It can be used in the main part of the session and at any time of the season.

Materials and equipment required: Two basketballs; one half court with one basket; four cones (floor markers); one stopwatch.

Coaching points: Players need to be encouraged to:

•   Take a good shot every time it's their turn – well balanced, with elbow under the ball, follow through.

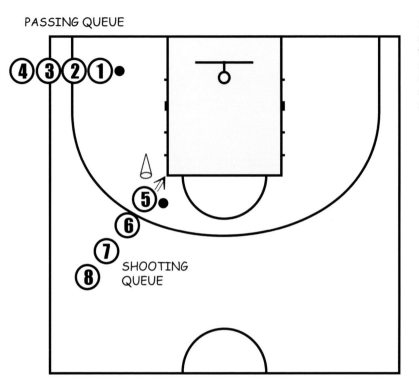

PASSING QUEUE

SHOOTING
QUEUE

Fig. 91 Five
minutes –
four spots
shooting drill
(continuation –
shooting from
second spot).

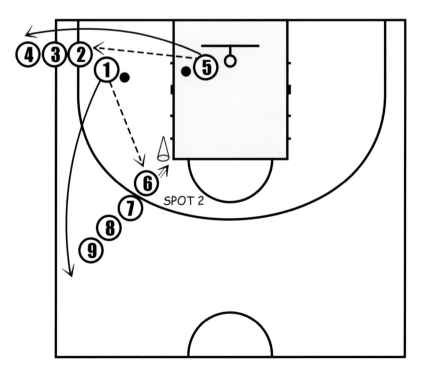

SPOT 2

Fig. 92 Five
minutes –
four spots
shooting drill
(continuation –
shooting from
second spot).

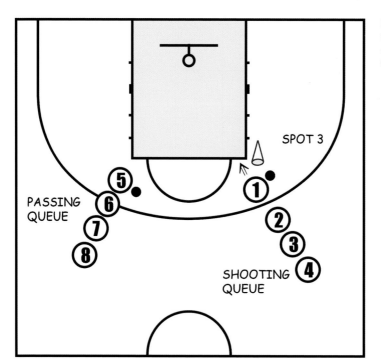

Fig. 93 Five minutes –
four spots shooting drill
(continuation – shooting
from third spot).

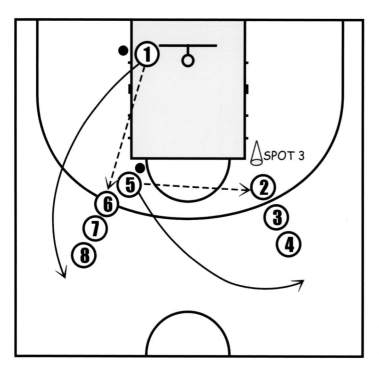

Fig. 94 Five minutes –
four spots shooting drill
(continuation – shooting
from third spot).

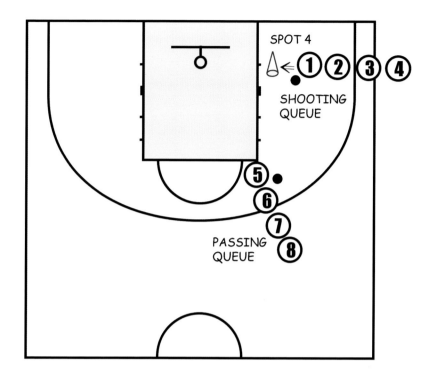

Fig. 95 Five minutes – four spots shooting drill (continuation – shooting from fourth spot).

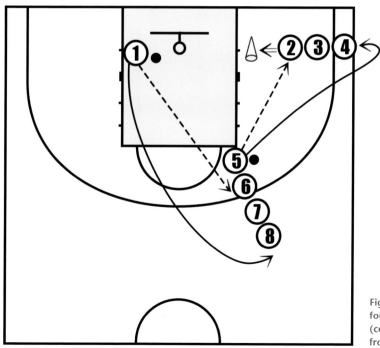

Fig. 96 Five minutes – four spots shooting drill (continuation – shooting from fourth spot).

- Go and rebound their own shot quickly and send an accurate and powerful pass to their teammate who is next in the passing queue (and also to the player who is next to shoot).
- Have their arms out in front of their chest, ready to catch and shoot, every time they are at the front of the shooting queue.

PROGRESSION:

- You can get the players to do this drill twice in a row – one time at one basket and then straight away, after ten to fifteen seconds change over (after a very short break) to the other basket at the other end of the court.

GO AROUND THE CONE SHOOTING DRILL (ON A HALF COURT)

Description: All players are in one queue close to one of the corners of the court (player 1 without a ball). One at a time, players will sprint towards the halfway line, go around the cone that is in front of them and will cut again, this time towards the basket in order to catch and shoot from midrange distance (see Fig. 97). After the cut and after going round the cone, player 1 will receive the ball from player 2 and will take the shot (catch and shoot action), then collect their own rebound and join the back of the queue behind player 4. After sending the pass to player 1, player 2 will start running straight away, will go round the cone and will receive from player 3 in order to take a jump shot. And the drill continues in a similar manner until the group scores 15 points (or 20, or a limit set up by coach) or they keep shooting for a certain time limit (one minute, two minutes and so on).

Use/purpose: The drill is used in order to employ a high number of shots; passes are

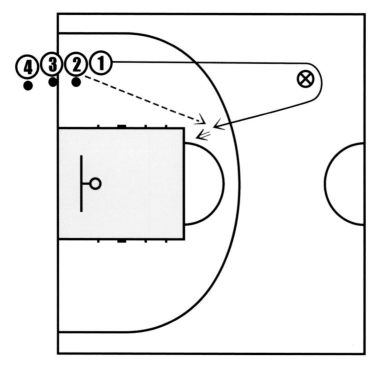

Fig. 97 Go around the cone shooting drill (on half court).

being practised too. Ability to catch and shoot is another outcome for this drill, together with the ability to stop instantly and shoot (footwork is also practised). It can be used in any part of the session (for example, could be a good warming-up exercise or as a shooting competition between two groups of players during the main part) and also in any part of the season.

Materials and equipment required: Three balls for four players; one half court with one basket; two cones.

Coaching points: Players need to be encouraged to:

- Leave their arm extended and follow through after each shot.
- Keep in mind the BEEF acronym and try to apply it – **B**alance (be well balanced when taking the shot), **E**lbow (have their elbow under the ball before they release the ball), **E**levation (lift the ball and extend

their arm), **F**ollow through (leave arm extended after releasing the ball).

- Cut powerfully towards the basket and do not stop before they receive the ball.
- Pass the ball on time to their teammate who is next to take the shot – do not delay the pass so that the drill is fluent, and the cut is effective.

PROGRESSION:

- Introduce a second cone (*see* Fig. 98). Player 1 starts without a ball in between the two cones; they will start by going round the second cone while at the same time player 2 (who does not have a ball) will perform a similar move around the first cone. Player 2 will receive from player 3 and, instead of shooting, 2 will now send an extra pass to 1 who by now should have finished their move around the cone – player 1 will catch and shoot.

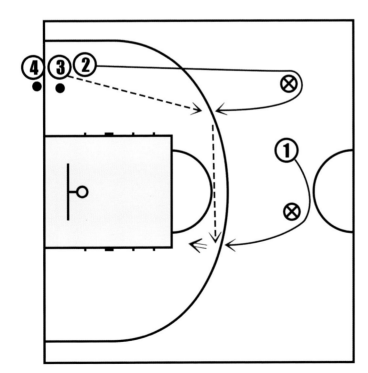

Fig. 98 Go around the cone shooting drill (on half court) – shooting after going round the second cone.

SHOOTING IN PAIRS (WITH OWN REBOUNDING) DRILL

Description: All players are grouped in pairs, with one ball between two players. As shown in Fig. 99, player 1 will take the shot from mid-range, goes and collects their own rebound, passes the ball to their partner and then joins the queue waiting their next turn (*see* Fig. 100). Player 2 will catch and shoot and the drill continues in this way until they score 10 points together as a pair (every time they score is 1 point) or whatever target the coach sets up (15, 20 and so on, depending on the ability and level of players).

Use/purpose: The drill is used primarily to take a high number of shots, practising in this way the fundamental element of shooting. Passing is practised too, along with the ability to go and rebound their own shot. It can be used in any part of a training session. With a small group of players it can be used as part of an individual workout.

Materials and equipment required: One ball between two players; one basket on half a court (you can have three to four pairs shooting at the same basket).

Coaching points: Players need to be encouraged to:

* Follow through – leave the arm extended after every shot.
* Be well balanced, with feet shoulder-width apart.
* Have their arms ready to catch the ball/the pass coming from their teammate.

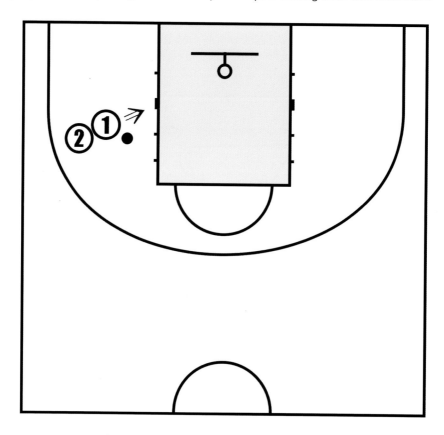

Fig. 99 Shooting in pairs (with own rebounding) drill.

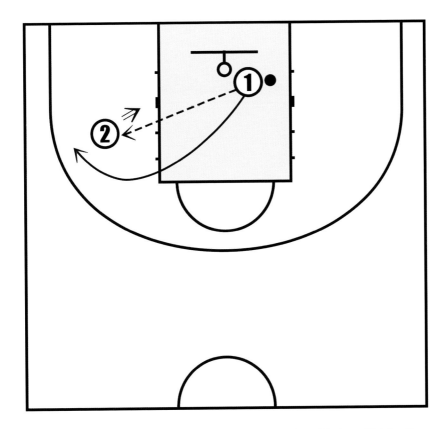

Fig. 100 Shooting in pairs (with own rebounding) drill – continuation with player 1 joining the queue.

- Jog/sprint to the back of the queue instead of walking.

PROGRESSION:
- Extend the distance and take the shots from 3 points semicircle (3 points shots).
- Add one fake and one quick dribble (right or left) so that they shoot off the dribble.
- Same drill but this time trying to score ten times as an individual player. The drill will stop when both have managed to score ten each – twenty in total; if one of them finished earlier than their team-mate then they keep shooting until they both finish.
- Same drill trying to score ten times together (or fifteen, twenty and so on) but this time when they miss four shots in a row, go back to zero – so, for example, if the players keep shooting and they made six and miss the next four shots, they go back to zero.

HOW TO ATTACK THE PICK AND ROLL 'ICE DEFENCE' DRILL

Description: One ball between two players and also a passing player (P) with a ball are needed for this drill – players 1 and 5 are attackers (1 is a playmaker or guard while 5 is a centre and they have the ball at the top of the key). There are three options for this drill.

Option 1: player 5 will pass to player 1 on the wing and then 5 will set a screen on the defender X1 who plays 'ice defence' – the defender is positioned with their body parallel with the sideline (see Fig. 101). This is when player 1 starts dribbling towards the corner/short corner area of court in order to create a 2 vs 1 situation: defender X5 will drop and position themselves very low on the baseline while attacker 5 sets the screen, holds the position (holds the defender) until 1 goes past them with the dribble and then 5 will roll to the basket (attackers 1 and 5 will create 2 vs 1 situation against defender X5). Player 1 will take a jump shot and 5 will receive the pass from P and will also take a jump shot.

Option 2: same principle to start the drill (5 passes to 1 and sets a screen on the defender X1 who is 'icing' the pick and roll). This time player 5 will roll wide towards the sideline after setting the screen and after player 1 uses the screen by dribbling out and then in (he 'snakes it' – the path resembles a snake). Player 1 will take a lay-up or a jump shot while 5 will receive the pass from P for a jump shot (note a different spot for P/where the pass is coming from for 5, see Fig. 102).

Option 3: same principle to start the drill (player 5 passes to player 1 and sets a screen on the defender who is 'icing' the pick and roll). This time player 5 will pop out towards the 3 points line after setting the screen and this is when player 1 will reverse the ball to

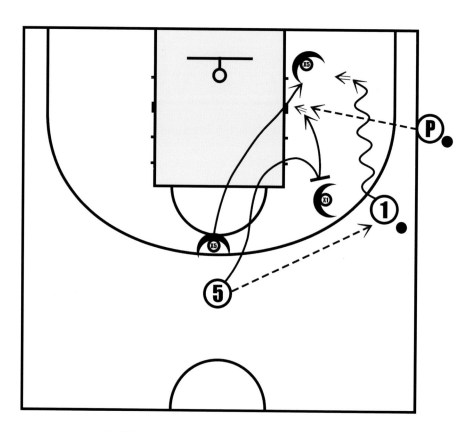

Fig. 101 How to attack the pick and roll 'ice defence' drill.

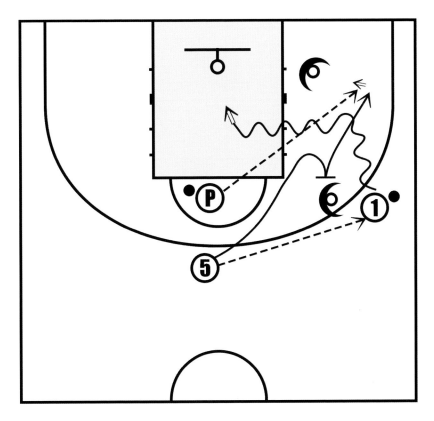

Fig. 102 How to attack the pick and roll 'ice defence' drill – option 2.

5 at the top of the key (*see* Figs. 103 and 104). After passing to 5, 1 will come at the top of the key for a hand off action, will receive the ball from 5 and will drive to the basket for a jump shot (or lay-up). Player 5 will roll, will receive from P and will shoot (note a different spot for P/where the pass is coming from for 5, *see* Fig. 105).

Use/purpose: This is primarily a shooting drill designed to take shots out a particular way to play in offence after using the pick and roll combination. While being a shooting drill, it is also useful for guards and centres to practise different options for how to attack out of a pick and roll situation and what to do. Dribbling is being worked on too (for guards) while ability to set a screen and to either roll to basket, short roll wide or pop out are also being practised.

Materials and equipment required: One ball between two players and one passing player with a ball; you can use two cones instead of defenders X1 and X5. One half court with one hoop.

Coaching points: Players need to be encouraged to:
- Be well balanced when taking a shot, with feet shoulder-width apart and follow through by leaving the arm extended.
- Send good, accurate passes.
- Keep their head up when dribbling.

PROGRESSION:
- Use semiactive defenders instead of cones (and instruct them not to block the shots taken by attackers).
- Repeat the drill on the other side of court.

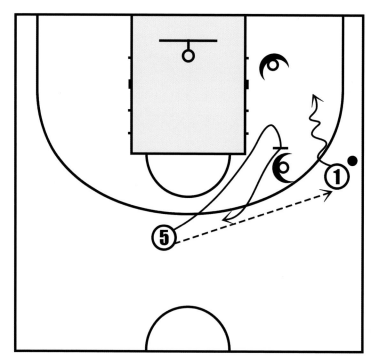

Fig. 103 How to attack the pick and roll 'ice defence' drill – centre sets a screen and pops out.

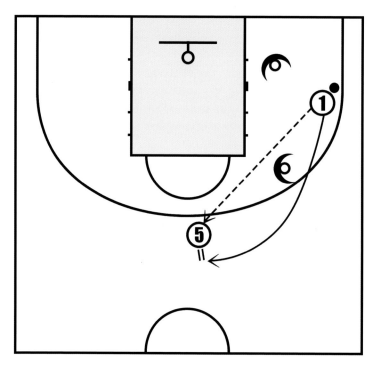

Fig. 104 How to attack the pick and roll 'ice defence' drill – guard passes and comes at the top of the key for a hand off action with centre.

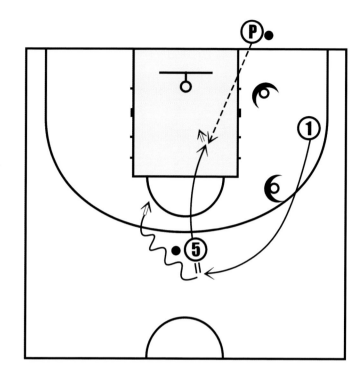

Fig. 105 How to attack the pick and roll 'ice defence' drill – guard drives to basket and centre rolls to basket to receive and shoot.

QUICK OFFENCE IN TWOS (WITH PASSING PLAYER IN THE MIDDLE) DRILL

Description: Each player has a ball; player 1 starts the drill from the free throw line extended just inside the 3 points semicircle while all remaining players will wait outside the court – they will pass to P (passing player or coach) and then will sprint on fastbreak towards the opposite basket by going wide, close to the sideline, around the cone that is on the halfway line (*see* Fig. 106). Player 1 will receive from P just around the other 3 points semicircle, will take one to two dribbles and will score a lay-up. Immediately after their shot, player 1 will rebound/collect the ball and will send a long pass straight to P inside the central circle; 1 will need to sprint again (wide, close to the side-line, around the cone) so that they now receive the pass just outside the key (elbow area), take one dribble and score a lay-up. As soon as

player 1 finishes their go, player 2 will continue the drill by doing the same.

Use/purpose: This is primarily a passing and shooting/finishing at the basket drill after sprinting full court. It can be used as a conditioning drill in pre-season, in season but also post season when you have a small number of players attending the session or for individualization.

Materials and equipment required: One ball per player; one full court with two hoops; two cones.

Coaching points: Players need to be encouraged to:
* Send strong, accurate passes.
* Focus on the lay-ups (try to make them).
* Dribble quickly and powerfully so that they do not slow down!

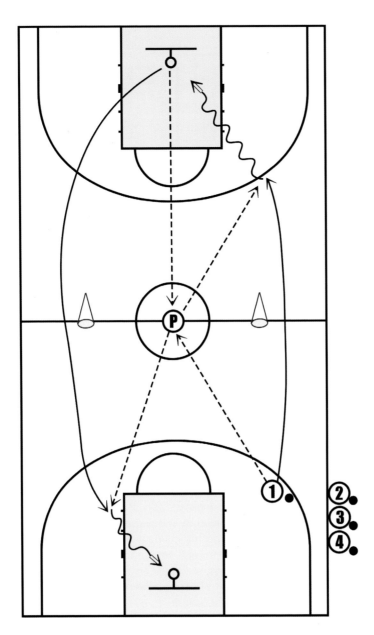

Fig. 106 Quick offence in twos (with passing player in the middle) drill.

- If they miss a lay-up, rebound and put it back.

PROGRESSION:
- Take a jump shot instead of a lay-up (at both ends).

- A passive defender could be introduced at one of the baskets.
- When working with more advanced players, each player can perform the drill twice in a row (four lengths of the court in total) without any stop in between.

TRANSITION SHOOTING DRILL (ON A HALF COURT)

Description: All players are lined up on the baseline, behind the basket, at point A on Fig. 107, while P1 and P2 are passing players (P1 in front of the basket ready to rebound and pass to P2; P2 at the elbow – they will always pass to the player whose turn it is/who is working). Player 1 will start the drill by going from cone A to cone B using defensive slides, then they will continue their move and sprint from B towards the halfway line; when they reach point C they will turn around and continue to run backwards up to cone D (to halfway line), then go around the cone and sprint towards the basket (facing the basket this time). At the cone that is at point E, they will receive the pass from P2 and will take a lay-up. Player 2 will start their go when player 1 goes around the halfway line (at point D). As a coach you can set a target – to score ten (or fifteen or twenty) as a whole group/team.

Use/purpose: This is a drill that combines shooting with defensive and offensive moves – in this way defensive slides, sprinting (while running forwards and backwards), cutting to basket, catching the ball on the move and shooting will all be practised. It can be used as part of the individualization process and also when coaching small groups of players before, during and after the season. This is a drill for guards and forwards primarily, however centres can also benefit from it.

Materials and equipment required: One ball; one half court with one basket; three cones.

Coaching points: Players need to be encouraged to:

- Stay low while doing the defensive slides; not crossing their legs.
- Be on their toes when sprinting – do not run flat-footed! Also to use their arms actively around their body for additional speed and balance.
- Sprint towards the basket (instead of an easy jog) and have their arms out ready to catch the ball.
- Take a good shot – be well balanced, have their feet shoulder-width apart and follow through (leave the arm extended).

PROGRESSION:

- Take a jump shot instead of a lay-up.
- When arriving at cone E, instead of catching the ball cut to the other side of the key and receive and shoot from there.

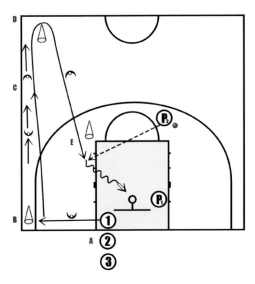

Fig. 107 Transition shooting drill (on half court).

DRILLS FOR DRIBBLING

DRIBBLING ACROSS THE COURT DRILL
(FROM FOUR QUEUES SET UP)

Description: All players are grouped in four queues, one in each corner of a half court (*see* Fig. 108). At the starting signal, players 1 and 7 will start dribbling the ball with the right hand diagonally across the court, as fast as they can, towards the opposite queue. As soon as players 1 and 7 start their first dribble, players 4 and 10 will start a similar action. When they

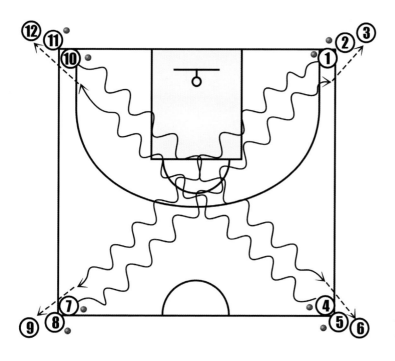

Fig. 108 Dribbling across the court drill (from four queues set-up).

arrive at the opposite queue, they will pass the ball to the player without the ball and join the back of the queue. At the next signal players 2 and 8, followed by players 5 and 11, will do the same and the drill continues in this manner. After a few reps with the right hand, ask players to do the same with left hand.

Use/purpose: The drill is used to develop and practise dribbling action/skills with both hands when there is no pressure from a defender. Players can start with an easy jog and then increase the speed while dribbling. It is useful with teams/groups that are big (twelve players or more).

Materials and equipment required: One ball per player ideally; one half court.

Coaching points: Players need to be encouraged to:

- Dribble to the side of the body, not in front of the feet.
- Keep their head up when dribbling.

- Control the ball constantly – do not slap the ball!
- Not catch the ball when they arrive in the middle for their stationary dribble.

PROGRESSION:

- Players 1 and 7 then 4 and 10 will start the dribbling action at the same time. When they meet in the middle, in order to avoid bumping into each other, they are required to dribble stationary with the right hand one time between their legs and continue their run towards the opposite queue with the left hand (*see* Fig. 109).
- Same as above but this time they start dribbling with the right hand, dribble stationary twice – once with the right hand between the legs then with the left hand crossed over, and continue their run with the right hand.

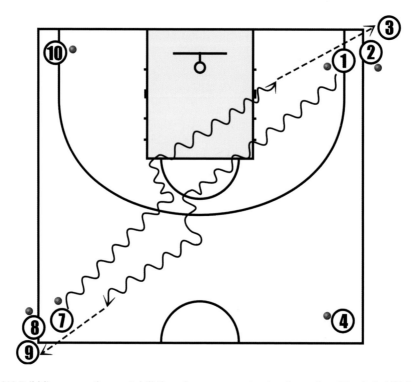

Fig. 109 Dribbling across the court drill (from four queues set-up) – players 1 and 7 switch dribbling hand.

CONTINUOUS DRIBBLING AROUND AND INSIDE THE 3 POINTS SEMICIRCLE DRILL

Description: Players are in groups of four to six players in one corner of a court with a ball each as illustrated in Fig. 110. Player 1 will start the drill by dribbling along the 3 points semicircle line with their left hand, using a sideways move/dribbling action. When they arrive in front of the first cone, they will attack the basket while dribbling until they reach the middle of the key (3–4m inside the key); performing a continuous dribbling action, they will then use a retreat dribble (dribble while moving backwards) so that they get back on the 3 points semicircle line where they will continue the dribbling action towards the next cone, where they will do the same – attack the basket followed by retreat dribble. After the last cone, they will go round the cone and after one or two dribbles player 1 will take a jump shot, will rebound their own shot and join the back of the queue where they started from. When player 1 is on their way to the second cone, player 2 will start their dribbling action and so on.

Use/purpose: The drill is asking players to use a variety of dribbling actions – dribble sideways, dribble forward (when attacking the basket), retreat dribble and so on. Court vision and ability to see the floor when dribbling are being developed at the same time. The drill can be used in the initial stages of learning to dribble the ball but also as a warm-up with players who have learnt this skill.

Materials and equipment required: One ball per player; three cones and one half of a court with clear markings for the 3 points semicircle.

Coaching points: Players need to be encouraged to:

- Use a continuous dribbling action – not to catch the ball with two hands until they reach the place from where they will shoot. During the drill they need to have

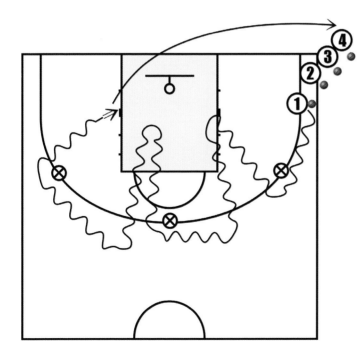

Fig. 110 Continuous dribbling around and inside the 3 points semicircle drill.

101

their body positioned so that they face the basket all the time (*see* Fig. 111).

- Keep their head up when dribbling so that they can see the whole floor.
- Not dribble the ball in front of their legs when attacking the basket.
- Control the ball constantly – do not slap the ball!

PROGRESSION:

- Dribbling and passing – same dribbling action to start off with but now a passing action can be added. The coach (or a passing player) is in the key and they will signal

a pass to the player who is dribbling. This player needs to send a pass exactly where the coach indicates – for example high, low or to the side. One hand pass can be used with more advanced players. The player will receive the pass back and will continue the dribbling action.

- A passive defender can be added next to each of the cones. The defender will shadow the dribbling player (during the attacking the basket moment and while the player uses the retreat dribble) without stealing the ball from the dribble but adding an element of pressure.

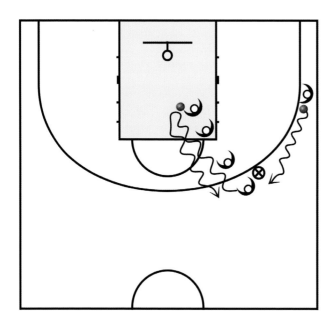

Fig. 111 Continuous dribbling around and inside the 3 points semicircle drill (note position of body while dribbling).

BALL DRIBBLING ON THE SPOT (STATIONARY DRIBBLING) DRILL

Description: One ball per player – all players are spaced out on court about 2–3m away from each other as seen in Fig. 112. The coach will give the signal for the start of the drill and players will dribble the ball on the spot for about thirty seconds or a minute, or for a certain number of bounces – perhaps twenty or thirty

dribbles. While being stationary, players will dribble as hard as they can in the following manner: they can start with a low dribble – this is when the ball will be kept below the knee level; very low dribble, below the ankles level (using 'baby' bounces); medium-height dribble when the ball does not go higher than the waist

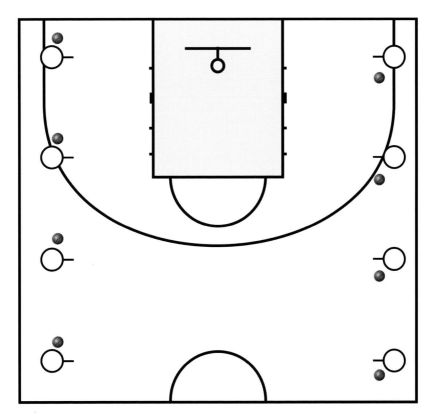

Fig. 112 Ball dribbling on the spot (stationary dribbling) drill.

level; high dribble with the ball below shoulder level; while sitting on the floor; while lying on the floor on their back; dribble somewhere next to their hips; and also while lying on the floor on their front; dribble in front of them, somewhere above their shoulders (see Fig. 113); dribble in front of their knees in a V-shape, similar to a crossover dribble; dribble between their legs; behind the back; other variations/combinations such as figure of eight between their legs, crossover followed by between the legs, crossover followed by between the legs followed by behind-the-back dribble.

Use/purpose: This type of drill improves control of the ball and enhances hand-eye co-ordination. It could be used as part of the warming up but also during the main part of a session when the aim is to work on dribbling.

Materials and equipment required: One ball per player; one half court.

Coaching points: Players need to be encouraged to:

- Push the ball hard into the floor and have their palm cushioning the ball when it bounces off the floor. Try not to dribble in front of their feet but slightly to the side.
- Have their fingers spread out each time the palm is in contact with the ball.
- Bend their knees, their hips, their ankles so that they are in a slightly flexed position (slightly leaning forward as opposed to standing upright, in a rigid position).
- Keep their head up when dribbling – not to look at the ball or at the floor in front of the feet.
- Control the ball (control the dribble) all the time.

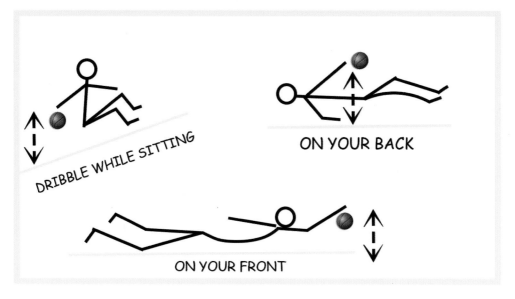

DRIBBLE WHILE SITTING

ON YOUR BACK

ON YOUR FRONT

Fig. 113 Ball dribbling on the spot while sitting and while lying on the back and on the front.

PROGRESSION:
- Change the hand they dribble with.
- From stationary dribbling go into dribbling while walking, easy jogging and running. Dribble while moving forwards and then dribble backwards.

- Dribble on the spot and then progress it onto dribbling while jogging and running, with two basketballs per player. Ask players to dribble both balls at the same time or as an alternative dribble – one ball going to the floor while the other one is coming up.

TAG WHILE DRIBBLING DRILL/FUN GAME

Description: All players are inside the basketball court and they all have a ball each. At the starting signal provided by the coach, perhaps a whistle or clap of hands, one of the players will be 'on' (coach's decision) and the task is to 'tag' another player while every single player involved, including the one who is chasing others, is dribbling with the right hand only so basically playing a game of 'tag' but always dribbling the ball (see Fig. 114). For example if player 1 has 'tagged' player 5, 5 will be the next player 'to be on' and 5 is not allowed to give it back to 1. If any of the players lose control of the ball while being chased, then

that player will be on. All the basketball rules with regards to travel, carried ball and double dribble will be followed and enforced; in addition, all players must stay inside the court and are not allowed to touch any of the sidelines or the baselines.

Use/purpose: A fun activity aimed to improve dribbling with both hands while jogging and running at different speeds (and with lots of changes of direction). The drill develops the ability to keep the head up while dribbling and also develops the decision-making when controlling the ball. It is great as a warm-up drill but also for during the main part of a session

Fig. 114 Tag while dribbling drill/fun game.

when trying to improve dribbling ability. It can be used in any part of the season.

Materials and equipment required: One ball per player; one full court with clear markings on.

Coaching points: Players need to be encouraged to:

- When tagging someone else, to try to be sensible and gentle; not to slap their teammates, push or trip others.
- Keep their head up when dribbling.
- Not dribble in front of their legs/feet – always slightly to the side.
- Not slap the ball when dribbling.

PROGRESSION:

- Ask players to use the left hand only (left-hand dribbling). Then ask them to dribble using either hand.
- Decrease the area where the game is being played – play on one half court only, for example.
- The same drill could be played in pairs in the following manner – tag in pairs while

dribbling (*see* Fig. 115). All players are grouped in pairs; one of them has the ball and will always dribble while the other one will just tag other pairs/other players when being 'on'. Two rules will always apply: the players need to hold hands all the time and the player with the ball needs to constantly dribble. If they do not hold hands when being chased and generally when running, then they will be on. Also, if a player in a pair loses control of the ball (for example if they stop dribbling by holding the ball, they dribble on their feet, they touch the sidelines and/or baselines) then they will be on. After one to two minutes, change the partner from the pair who is dribbling the ball. This version of the game requires working together as a pair/as a team so that both partners in the pair will go in the same direction when running away from the chasers or they both go for the same pair when they are on and chase others.

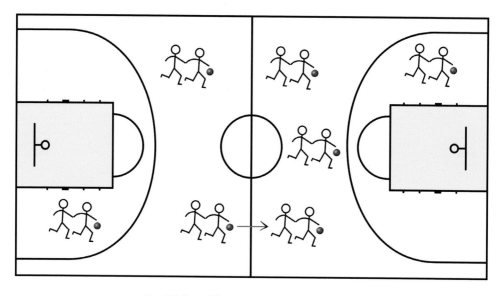

Fig. 115 Tag while dribbling in pairs (*fun game*).

1 vs 1 FULL COURT AFTER DRIBBLING PLAYER CHANGES DIRECTION

Description: Players will work in pairs: player 1 is attacker (and has the ball) while player 2 is a defender. Both of them start outside the court on either side of halfway line (*see* Fig. 116). At a starting signal, they both start running towards the middle of court; player 1 starts by dribbling towards the central circle – the rule is that they need to have at least one foot in the circle and from here they will decide which way to go, to either the basket on the right or on the left, in order to dribble and take a lay-up. As soon as player 1 starts their move from the sideline, player 2 will also start sprinting towards the middle in order to defend and try and stop player 1 from scoring. In this way they play 1 vs 1 towards one of the baskets (the one that is chosen by the dribbling player) – for example towards basket B as in Fig. 116. Once players 1 and 2 finish their 1 vs 1 game, the next pair will have their turn.

Use/purpose: The drill is used to develop players' ability to dribble quickly towards the basket and score while being under the pressure of a defender (while being closely guarder by the defender). Decision-making and reaction are also worked on alongside the ability to play defence in a 1 vs 1 situation on full court. The drill can be used in the main part of a session.

Materials and equipment required: One ball between two players; one full court with two baskets.

Coaching points: Players need to be encouraged to:

- Not dribble the ball in front of their legs.
- When sprinting and dribbling towards the basket, to use a medium or high dribble so that they can dribble at speed.
- As defenders, try to stop the drive, put pressure on the attacker and also try to block their shot. Make sure they box out after the shot is taken!

PROGRESSION:

- Player 1 is allowed to use one direction fake and in this way change their direction

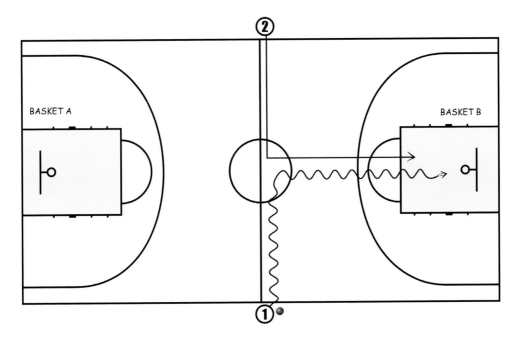

Fig. 116 1 vs 1 full court after dribbling player changes direction.

before going to the basket for a lay-up in order to deceive their defender. So for example player 1 starts by going to basket A after getting out of the central circle and they can change their direction by suddenly going to basket B.

• Play another 1 vs 1 game on a full court after the first action is over – player 1 will become defender and player 2 will be the new attacker (and try to score at the other basket this time).

8 | DRILLS FOR REBOUNDING

THROW THE BALL AND REBOUND INDIVIDUALLY DRILL

Description: Each player has a ball and is lined up on the baseline (*see* Fig. 117). At the starting signal, they all start jogging forward towards the other end line of court. Individually, each player will throw the ball high in the air (about 2–3m ahead of them and about 4–5m high) and then they will jump to catch the ball in the air (*see* Fig. 117) and then land on both feet with the ball in their hands. There are four places on the court where they perform this move (the dotted lines in Fig. 117). The focus is on a powerful jump, on catching the ball in the air and on landing while holding the ball with two hands (catching the ball with two hands and landing on both feet is highly recommended; also, keep the ball at your chin level).

Use/purpose: This is a preliminary exercise to get players used to the idea that they have to jump in order to get the rebound. It exercises the basic moves that are needed when rebounding a ball, such as jumping, catching the ball while being in the air or landing.

Materials and equipment required: One ball per player; one full court.

Coaching points: Players need to be encouraged to:

- Keep an eye on the ball while it is still in the air.

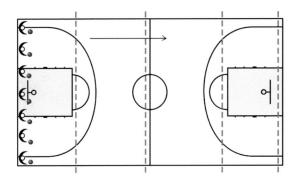 

Fig. 117 Throw the ball and rebound individually drill.

- Fully extend their arms towards the ball in order to meet it early, in the air.
- Land with feet shoulder-width apart, while holding the ball with both hands in front of their shoulders.
- Not get the ball below their shoulders, towards their waist (or below).
- Jump powerfully up in the air to meet/ catch the ball.

PROGRESSION:
- Throw the ball high, let it bounce only once somewhere in front of them and then sprint to collect it (the idea behind this action being to rebound a ball that gets on the floor).

THROW AND CATCH YOUR PARTNER'S BASKETBALL

Description: In pairs, each player has a ball. Players 1 and 2 work together at one end of the court while players 3 and 4 will do the same coming from the opposite end of court. All other players are lined up behind them (*see* Fig. 118). Player 1 will throw the ball high up in the air (about 4–5m high and about 2–3m ahead) and then immediately sprint to rebound/to get the ball that was thrown high by their partner (player 2). At the same time, player 2 will do the same – throw their ball up high (forward and upwards) so that player 1 can come and rebound it while they (2) will go to rebound player 1's ball. They will continue doing so until they arrive at the other end of court. When players 1 and 2 go over the halfway line, players 5 and 6 will start their turn (the same for players 7 and 8 – who will start when 3 and 4 are over the halfway line).

Use/purpose: The drill develops the ability to locate the ball in the air and to synchronize their own moves (jump to get the rebound) with the path/flight of the ball. Ability to jump and to catch the ball in the air is also being practised. Apart from this, focus, concentration and co-operation are required – advise players to avoid each other when going to get the rebound.

Materials and equipment required: One ball for each player; one full court.

Coaching points: Players need to be encouraged to:
- Extend arms fully when getting the ball.
- Keep an eye on the ball all the time.

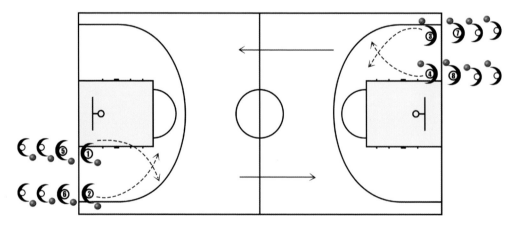

Fig. 118 Throw and catch your partner's basketball.

- Catch the ball with both hands and bring it to their chest/chin as soon as they can on landing.

- .Throw the ball high, give a 'high five' to their partner and catch the ball.

THROW THE BALL ONTO BACKBOARD AND GET THE REBOUND DRILL

Description: Each player has a ball and is situated at about 3–4m away from the basket (the ideal scenario would be to have a minimum of five to six baskets around the sports hall so that two to three players can work at one basket). In turn, each player throws the ball onto the board (*see* Fig. 119) and then sprints to the basket in order to jump and catch the ball while it is still in the air, then land on both feet. After rebounding and landing, the player will take a jump shot straight away (in case of a missed shot, they will rebound again and shoot from where they got the rebound until they make the shot).

Use/purpose: The drill develops the ability of a player to rebound a ball that bounces off the backboard. Attention and concentration to time their own jump with the flight of the ball are also being practised.

Materials and equipment required: One ball per player; a minimum of five to six baskets around the court.

Coaching points: Players need to be encouraged to:
- Not jump until the ball has left the backboard.
- Jump upwards in order to catch the ball while their body is in the air and keep an eye on the ball all the time.
- Fully extend their arms in order to reach the ball while it is in the air.
- Land on both feet and keep their feet shoulder-width apart for good balance.

Fig. 119 Throw the ball onto the backboard and get the rebound drill.

Maintain a balanced position on landing by flexing their knees, ankles and hips.

- Put two hands on the ball and protect it as soon as they land.

PROGRESSION:

- Same drill as above but this time rebound the ball, land on both feet, spin around (360 degrees) with the help of a powerful dribble and shoot the ball from the other side of the ring.

- Two teams of five to six players each are lined up in front of the basket. One player at a time will throw the ball onto the board so that the player behind comes and jumps to rebound the ball in the air and throws in again on the board for the next player and so on. After they catch and throw the ball, they should immediately go and join the back of the queue so that the drill continues and flows without interruptions.

THROW THE BALL ONTO THE BACKBOARD ABOVE THE RING AND GET THE REBOUND DRILL

Description: Each player with a ball, on one side of the basket (to the side of the ring). Individually, one player at a time, throw the ball onto the board (above the ring) and sprint to get the rebound from the other side of the ring (*see* Fig. 120). As soon as they get the rebound, land on both feet and then take a jump shot immediately.

Use/purpose: This drill is used to practise getting the rebound while the ball is in the air and to actively jump to get it. It develops a feel and the anticipation for where the ball will bounce off. Very useful, especially for centres to develop their ability to rebound.

Materials and equipment required: One ball per player; one basket on a half court.

Coaching points: Players need to be encouraged to:

- Time their jump accurately so that they do not jump too early or too late. Also, make

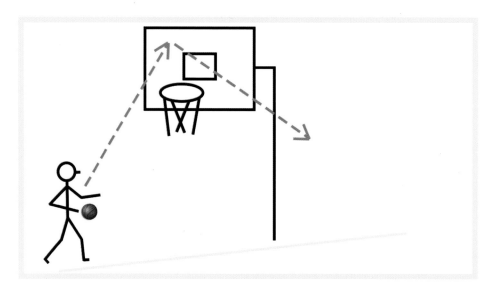

Fig. 120 Throw the ball onto the backboard above the ring and get the rebound drill.

sure they jump instead of waiting on the ground for the ball to get to them.

- Keep an eye on the ball all the time.
- Catch the ball with both hands and bring it to their chest/chin as soon as they can on landing.
- Fully extend arms in order to reach the ball while it is in the air.
- When landing, land on both feet and keep their feet shoulder-width apart for good balance. Maintain a balanced position on landing by flexing their knees, ankles and hips.

PROGRESSION:
- The player will catch the ball, will perform a shooting fake and then will take a reverse lay-up (a shot from the other side of the ring).
- A defender is situated on the free throw line – they become active and try to block the shot/plays defence as soon as the ball is being thrown onto the board.

FIGHT FOR THE REBOUND DRILL

Description: Groups of four players in front of one basket: one player is getting ready to take a jump shot from the free throws line area while the other three are in the key, just in front of the basket (*see* Fig. 121). The aim of the drill is for one of the three players in the key to get the rebound when their teammate takes a shot – they try to get the rebound while 'fighting' with and against the other players. Who gets the rebound goes to the free throw line and replaces that player who now will become one of the rebounders. The drill can be played until one player gets a specific number of rebounds.

Use/purpose: The drill is trying to get players used to the idea that they have to 'fight' for the rebound and to jump while other players are doing the same thing. Good leg strength is being developed so players can stay strong on their feet, to help jump to collect the ball.

Materials and equipment required: One ball and one basket.

Coaching points: Players need to be encouraged to:
- Try to keep an eye on the ball while locating where the other two players are.
- Box out one of the other rebounders in order to secure a clear jump and catch the ball.
- Time their jump accurately so that they do not jump too early or late. Also, make sure they jump instead of waiting on the ground for the ball to get to them.
- When landing, land on both feet and keep their feet shoulder-width apart for good balance.

PROGRESSION:
- Once they get the rebound, play 'live' trying to score against the other two players who become defenders. Play until a basket is scored or the ball goes out of bounds.

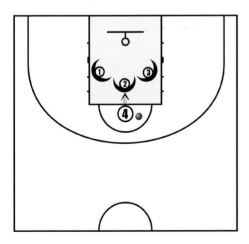

Fig. 121 Fight for the rebound drill.

DRILLS FOR DEFENCE

This sub-chapter will contain individual and team defence exercises (for both half court and full court playing situations during the game). Apart from being heavily influenced by the physical abilities of the player (for example in terms of speed, agility, balance), defence is more importantly about the desire and the willingness to work hard and to put in an effort, about the determination and concentration for the duration of the defensive moment (perhaps twenty-four seconds, a whole quarter or a full game). A general proactive attitude towards defence (and towards playing defence) is to be encouraged by coaches – lots of coaches nowadays prefer players who are good defenders at the expense of players who are good only when playing offence; playing good defence will allow your team to limit the scoring opportunities of the opposition by forcing turnovers, by getting defensive rebounds, by getting steals and interceptions, by gaining possessions that then will facilitate easy scoring opportunities such as fastbreaks, quick offences, easy basket/points. The word *proactive* is the key when playing defence; as a defender you need to be proactive and dictate the play, dictate the way you want your team and the opposition to play, to the extent that you almost impose your way of playing defence to the opposition instead of allowing them to have the initiative – force them to take bad shots (contested shots), do not give unguarded lay-ups nor open shots, force them to play the ball onto a particular area of the court (for example in the corners in order to trap), have a plan for how to play against their screens, limit their penetration and cuts and so on. Do not forget to celebrate when you have success in defence – exactly as you do in offence when you score points and celebrate you can do the same for the defensive moments!

As a general piece of advice when teaching defence – coaches need to reinforce several principles such as active hands, active feet, together with active eyes and active mouths. The reasons why are simple: having active hands will make it difficult for an attacker to pass, to dribble or even to shoot (you can steal the ball from the dribble, you can prevent a pass, you can block a shot, you can deny a pass onto your player, and so on); having active feet will allow you as a defender to move quickly and efficiently everywhere on the court when playing defence; having active eyes is equally important because as a defender you need to be in a position to be aware and to see what happens on the court (such as the position of a direct opponent, position of teammates, of opposite players) and even possibly to anticipate certain moves and actions from the opposition, which will enable you to make better decisions (such as shall I stay with my player, shall I go, shall I switch?), while loud, clear verbal communication is categorically needed and gives your team a small advantage over the opposition – teams that are constantly talking and communicating when playing defence are always more effective than those that are very quiet!

TRANSITION DEFENCE (1 vs 0 THEN 2 vs 1) DRILL

Description: Players are divided into groups of three and they start the drill as follows: player 1 with the ball is initially an attacker and starts just below the free throw line (outside the key) as in Fig. 122; while players 2 and 3 are defenders and they start on the baseline, so that in this way player 1 has a small advantage. Player 1 starts the drill and will sprint towards basket A in order to score a lay-up. Players 2 and 3 will chase them trying to catch and block the shot (or stop the drive). After player 1 takes the lay-up (made shot or missed), 2 and 3 will get the rebound (or inbound the ball in case of a made shot) and will play 2 vs 1 (players 2 and 3 against player 1) towards the other basket, basket B (see Fig. 123). Player 1 will need to sprint again – back in defence this time – so that players 2 and 3 do not score an easy lay-up.

Use/purpose: The drill practises transition back into defence and also defence against two attackers (numerical superiority/advantage). Ability to dribble at speed and under the pressure of a defender coming from behind gets to be exercised too. The drill is usually used in the beginning parts of a session when the body is not tired, for sprinting purposes.

Materials and equipment required: One ball between three players; one full court with two baskets.

Coaching points:
- Player 1 (initially with the ball) needs to sprint twice – once in offence (while dribbling, trying to score) and once back in defence. Sprinting action is recommended for players 2 and 3 to get back in defence

(when they go towards basket A) but also on fastbreak as part of the 2 vs 1 action.
- Player 1 needs to dribble at speed – the dribbling action is a bit higher than usual but below the shoulder level.

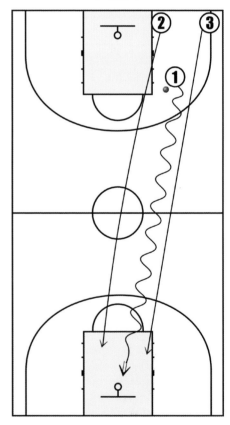

BASKET B

BASKET A

Fig. 122 Transition defence (1 vs 0 then 2 vs 1) drill.

- For players 2 and 3 – rebound (or inbound) the ball quickly and start the 2 vs 1 action immediately.
- Player 1 – sprint back in defence and then actively wait for the two attackers (2 and 3) above the free throw line level.

PROGRESSION:
- The drill can start with four players initially (instead of three) – players 2, 3 and 4 will get back in defence initially and then on the way back it is a 3 vs 1 action instead of 2 vs 1 as before (*see* Fig. 124). Players 2, 3 and 4 will play against 1.
- Another defender can be introduced on the way back – player 5 (who is waiting on the side of the court at the free throw line extended level) will wait for teammate 1 to sprint and take the lay-up; and, as soon as one of the players 2, 3 or 4 will get the rebound or inbound the ball, will go round the cone then sprint back in defence (*see* Fig. 125). In this way the drill becomes 3 vs 1+1/3 vs 2 eventually

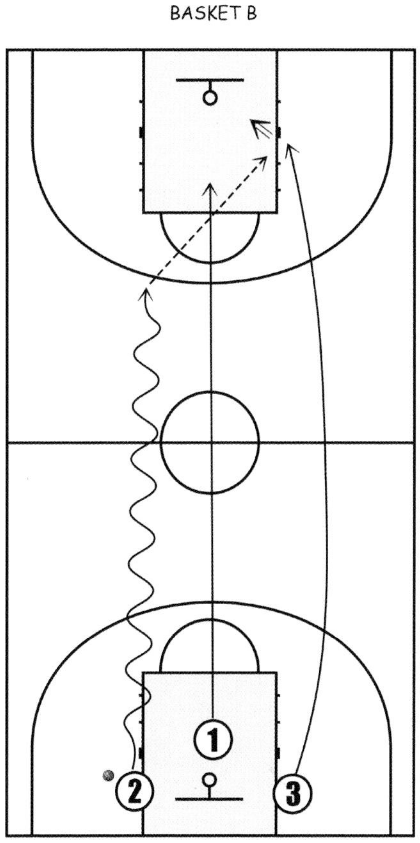

BASKET B

Fig. 123 Transition defence (1 vs 0 then 2 vs 1) drill – continuation with players 2 and 3 attacking against player 1.

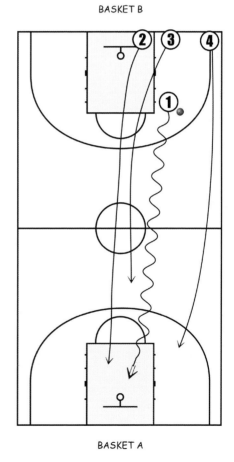

BASKET B

BASKET A

Fig. 124 Transition defence (1 vs 0 then 2 vs 1) drill – with four players (and 3 vs 1 action on the way back).

BASKET B

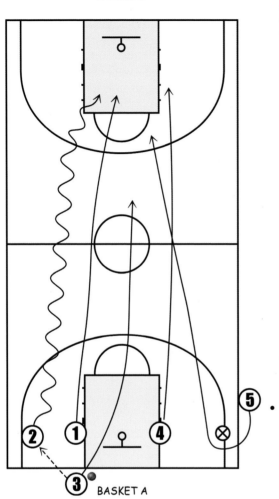

BASKET A

Fig. 125   Transition defence (1 vs 0 then 2 vs 1) drill – progression with an additional defender waiting on the sideline (and 3 vs 2 action on the way back).

(players 2, 3 and 4 initially against player 1 and against player 5 too once player 5 got back in defence).
• Ask the players 2, 3 and 4 not to dribble when they become attackers (on the way to basket B as part of the 2 vs 1 and as part of the 3 vs 1 +1 action) so that they play in offence without dribbling!

1 vs 1 ON A HALF COURT AND THEN ON FULL COURT AFTER OUTLET PASS DRILL

Description: The drill starts with three players who are positioned as in Fig. 126 – player A with the ball at the top of the key, then player B in offence and player X1 defending player B (with both of them in the low post area). Player B will get open so that they receive from A on the wing (see Fig. 126). Once they receive the ball, player B will play 1 vs 1 against X1 (see Fig. 127) until they (player B) scores or until X1 gets the ball, for example as a consequence of a blocked shot, rebound, steal, or after the basket is scored. When X1 gets the ball, as a consequence of any of the actions described previously, after the 1 vs 1 play, player A will sprint to the opposite wing (below the free throw line extended) in order to receive an outlet pass from X1 or an inbound pass if the basket was made (*see* Fig. 128). At this moment the drill becomes 1 vs 1 on full court – 1 vs 1 action between player A who now has the ball against player B who needs to sprint back in defence to stop and prevent a fastbreak and a shot (lay-up preferably) from A (*see* Fig. 129). Player B does not have time

to rest after they play 1 vs 1 on a half court against X1 (they score or miss the shot) – they will need to sprint back in defence immediately! The drill continues until A scores or until B gets the ball, for example after a rebound, steal or blocked shot.

Use/purpose: The drill is used to practise (and eventually get better at) playing offence and then immediately having to sprint back in defence – so quick thinking and decision-making are required. Defence is being practised too with players X1 and B having to work hard in order to stop the attacking action. Ability to play 1 vs 1 (both in offence and in defence) is also developed.

Materials and equipment required: One ball between three players; one full court with a basket at each end of the court.

Coaching points:

- A good defensive action is required initially – player X1 does not allow player B to catch the ball easily! Once B has got the ball, X1 needs to maintain the same defensive pressure on their opponent – low stance, active feet and active hands to prevent them from scoring.

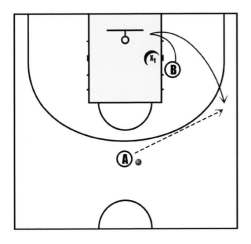

Fig. 126 1 vs 1 on half court and then on full court after outlet pass drill – player B receives on the wing from A.

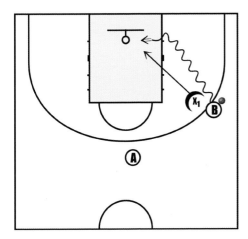

Fig. 127 1 vs 1 on half court and then on full court after outlet pass drill – player B plays against X1.

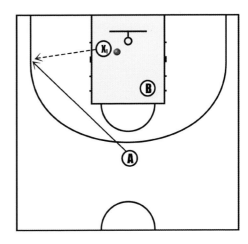

Fig. 128 1 vs 1 on half court and then on full court after outlet pass drill – X1 outlet pass to player A.

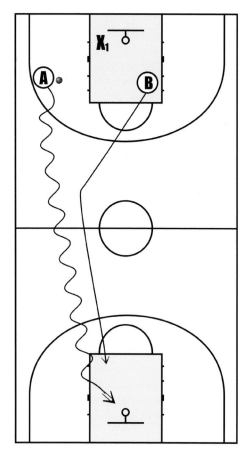

Fig. 129 1 vs 1 on half court and then on full court after outlet pass drill – 1 vs 1 action on full court (A plays against B).

- For the initial 1 vs 1 action – it is important to take a good shot, which could be a lay-up or a jump shot (for player B).
- It has to be a sprint back in defence for player B once X1 sends the outlet pass to A.
- For player B – when playing full court defence against A – come and meet the ball early so that A does not have an easy (unguarded) lay-up.

PROGRESSION:

- For the initial 1 vs 1 action on a half court – player B has two or three dribbles maximum in order to get a shot.
- At the end of the 1 vs 1 action on full court (player A against player B), player B can take the ball and play again 1 vs 1 on full court against player A (in this way they will be a defender and then immediately they become an attacking player).

DEFENCE STAYS ON COURT DRILL

Description: This is a drill for twelve players (three teams of four players) but it can work with minimum nine players too (three teams of three players). Team A (players A1, A2, A3 and A4) is on the court, has the ball and is ready to play offence 4 vs 4 against Team X (X1, X2, X3 and X4) who is waiting at the opposite basket (Team X defends basket A) as illustrated in Fig. 130. Team B (players B1, B2, B3 and B4) are waiting their turn on baseline under basket B – passing player P1 will pass the ball to them

as soon as the first 4 vs 4 game is over – as in Fig. 131. Team A plays 4 vs 4 against Team X on a half court. There are two situations:

Situation 1: If Team A scores (see Figs 131 and 132), then Team A will become defenders waiting for Team B to come at the same basket to play against each other on a half court. At the same time, Team X will jog on the sideline back in the queue behind Team B, who have now gone onto the other court to play Team B against Team A (see Fig. 132).

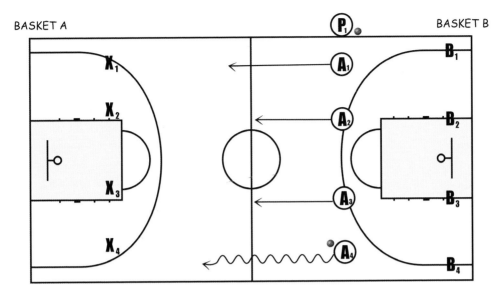

Fig. 130 Defence stays on court drill – team A ready to play against team X.

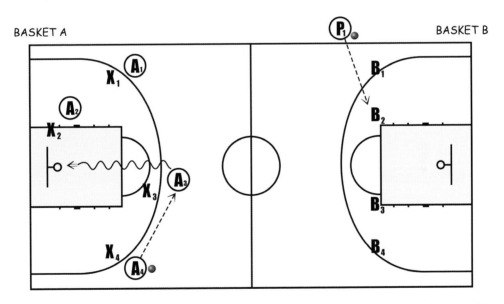

Fig. 131 Defence stays on court drill – team B ready to start after receiving the ball from passing player P.

Situation 2: If Team X gets a defensive stop (they prevent Team A from scoring by playing good defence and they eventually get the ball), then Team A will get out of the court and will jog to the other end of court (to basket B) to join the queue and wait for their turn (see Fig. 133). In this instance, Team B will attack and play against Team X (Team B in offence, Team X in defence).

The actions (the 4 vs 4 play and the transition into offence) have to be quick – all the changes

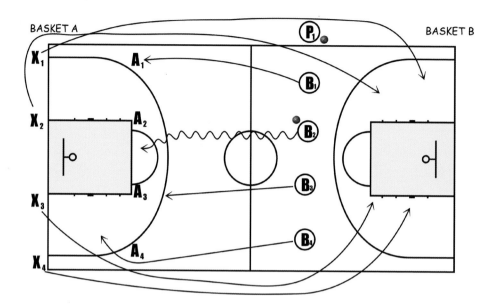

Fig. 132 Defence stays on court drill – team B ready to play against team A if team A scores.

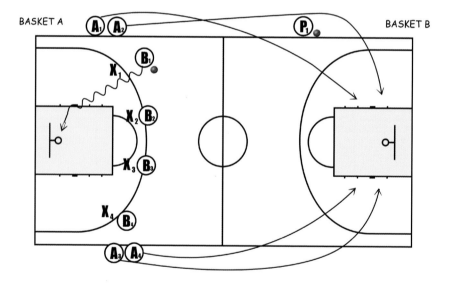

Fig. 133 Defence stays on court drill – team B ready to play against team X if team A fails to score.

from defence out of court (if you get scored against), from offence to defence (if you score) must be quick and passing player P has to pass the ball pretty quickly to the team waiting at basket B, so the players in defence (at basket A) need to get their defence organized early.

Use/purpose: The main aim of the drill is to play good defence and try and get a defensive stop (for example a defensive rebound, a steal or force a turnover – this is when the 4 vs 4 action stops and another team joins the action) and in this way to stay on the court, as opposed to leaving the court and joining the back of the queue while waiting for another turn. The drill develops quick thinking and decision-making. Certain set plays can be practised too during the 4 vs 4 play (for both offence and for defence).

Materials and equipment required: Two balls; one full court with a basket at each end. Twelve players ideally (or more) but the drill can work with nine players too.

Coaching points:

- When receiving the ball from passing player P and coming from basket B to basket A, players need to immediately pass the ball to their playmaker and get the offence organized (call a play, for example).

- Each player needs to know who they are guarding from the other two teams and get their defence sorted as soon as the 4 vs

4 game is over – this is because the other team waiting in the queue is coming to play quickly!

- Half court defence principles need to be implemented/followed: pressure on the ball, deny first pass, prevent the cuts and the drives, box out after every shot, get the rebound – depending on what you as a coach want your team to play in defence (your defensive principles).

PROGRESSION: The drill and the 4 vs 4 play can be restricted/conditioned in following ways:

- Ask the attacking team to play offence without dribble – so they cannot dribble when in offence.

- Once in offence on a half court, the attacking team has fourteen seconds only to take the shot.

DEFENCE IN 1 vs 1 SITUATION (AGAINST MULTIPLE ATTACKERS) DRILL

Description: Player A (who is a defender) starts the drill under the basket while players 1, 2 and 3 (who are attackers) are positioned around the 3 points semicircle (*see* Fig. 134). Player A has a ball and will start the drill by passing the ball to player 1. After the pass, A will sprint to defend 1. Player 1, who now has the ball, will wait for A to get close, within arm's length, and then will play 1 vs 1 (1 against A) at that basket (*see* Fig. 135). This first 1 vs 1 action will stop when the defender A gets the ball, as a consequence of a steal, defensive rebound or after the basket is scored, or when the attacker scores. The drill continues immediately with A who will get the ball and pass it directly to player 2 who is waiting on 3 points line semicircle and A will now sprint to defend 2; meanwhile player 1 will go back to the initial spot they occupied (*see* Fig. 136). Player A now plays defence against player 2 who will attack trying to

score (*see* Fig. 137). Once the action between player 2 and A is over (basket is scored or A gets possession), A will continue the drill by

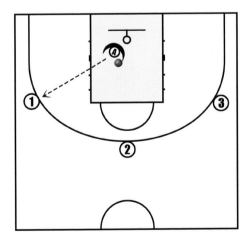

Fig. 134 Defence in 1 vs 1 situation (against multiple attackers) drill.

passing the ball straight away, without any break, to player 3 and by sprinting to get in a defensive position (*see* Fig. 138), player 2 will get back to where they started – at the top of the key. Player A will now defend player 3, trying to stop them from scoring (*see* Fig. 139). Once all these three actions are over, players will rotate so that now player 1 becomes a defender (and goes under the basket) and A will replace player 1, becoming an attacking player and so on.

Use/purpose: The drill is getting players to work in defence in a 1 vs 1 situation on a half court. It encourages multiple efforts from the defender in their attempt to stop the attacker from scoring, as part of the three consecutive actions. The drill can be used in the main part of the session after a good warming up or even

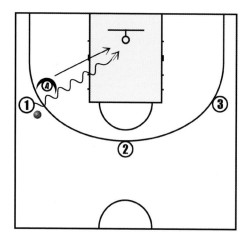

Fig. 135 Defence in 1 vs 1 situation (against multiple attackers) drill – player 1 plays against defender A.

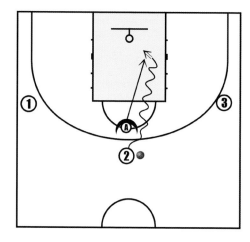

Fig. 137 Defence in 1 vs 1 situation (against multiple attackers) drill – player 2 plays against defender A.

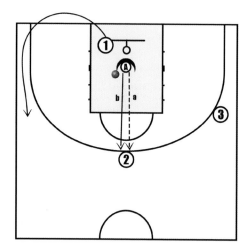

Fig. 136 Defence in 1 vs 1 situation (against multiple attackers) drill – player A passes the ball to player 2 (while 1 gets back to their spot).

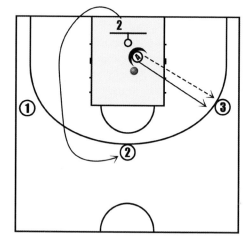

Fig. 138 Defence in 1 vs 1 situation (against multiple attackers) drill – player A passes the ball to player 3 (while 2 gets back to their spot).

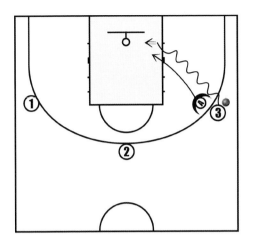

Fig. 139 Defence in 1 vs 1 situation (against multiple attackers) drill – player 3 plays against defender A.

in the later stages of the session when players are tired and they still need to concentrate and play hard in defence.

Materials and equipment required: One ball; one basket on a half court (with court markings visible).

Coaching points: Players need to be encouraged to:

- For defender A:
  - o   Sprint to the attacker in order to close out after sending the pass.
  - o   Have and maintain a low defending position, with feet wide, knees bent/ flexed, ready to react to the attacker's moves.
  - o   Try to keep the ball between their feet all the time.

- o   Have active hands – one hand up to prevent the shot and one low to try and disturb the dribble. Active hands and active feet defence!
- o   Keep the attacker out of the paint and force them to take a bad shot (ideally from outside the key). Box out after the shot so that they secure the rebound – do not give second chance points.
- For attackers (1, 2 and 3): use a maximum of two to three dribbles per possession in order to get close to the basket and score a lay-up (preferably).

PROGRESSION:

- Ask attackers to use one or two dribbles maximum before they take the shot.
- After an attacking player gets the offensive rebound and scores, defender A will come back again to this attacker (by passing the ball to them) and play 1 vs 1 defence again. For example if attacker 1 rebounds and scores, defender A will pass to 2 and then to 3 and afterwards A will pass once more to player 1, to play against them again.
- During the drill, any player might decide to pass the ball to a teammate on the 3 points semicircle. So for example, player 1 might decide to pass the ball to player 2 instead of attacking the basket against A. This is when A will go to where the pass goes and play defence against that attacker.

1 vs 1 AFTER THREE PASSES DRILL

Description: In pairs, one ball between two players. Player 1 starts the drill by passing to player 2 on their way to the other basket (*see* Fig. 140). After three passes, the drill becomes 1 vs 1 live, with player 2 becoming attacker and 1 being the defender. They play until player 2 scores (or loses the ball) or until player 1 gets a defensive stop (such as a defensive rebound, blocks the shot or steals the ball).

Use/purpose: Ability to defend in 1 vs 1 situation on a half court is being worked on. The drill can be used during the main part

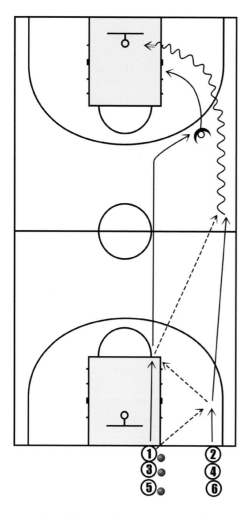

Fig. 140 1 vs 1 after three passes drill.

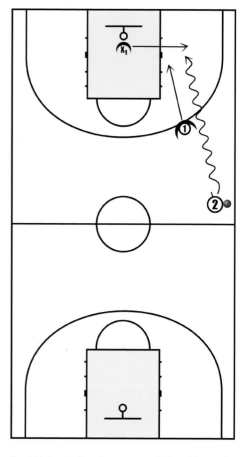

Fig. 141 1 vs 1 after three passes drill – with another defender included in the drill.

of a session (during the various stages of a season).

Materials and equipment required: One ball; one full court.

Coaching points: Players need to be encouraged to:

- Put pressure on the attacking player right outside the 3 points semicircle by having active feet and active hands (stay low on their feet, with arms wide open). Do not allow the attacking player to drive through the middle of the court (do not give the middle) – force them sideline–baseline.
- For the attacker: protect the ball with the non-dribbling hand and with the foot/body.

PROGRESSION:

- Add another defender who waits under the basket and who will come to help when the attacker drives sideline–baseline (*see* Fig. 141).

2 vs 2 CONTINUOUS DRILL ON A HALF COURT

Description: Players 1 and 2 are attackers while X1 and X2 are defenders. The drill starts with player 3 who will pass the ball to 1. When 1 receives the ball, 1 will play 2 vs 2 on a half court together with 2 against X1 and X2 (*see Fig. 142*). Players 3 and 5 will replace 1 and 2 on the halfway line (they will wait their turn at both ends of it) and they will be the new attackers once the initial 2 vs 2 action is over. When player 1 drives against X1, defender X2 needs to be on the imaginary middle line of the court (the dotted line in Fig. 143) so that they can help X1 in their attempt to stop attacker 1 from scoring. Once 1 and 2 finish their action (score or lose the possession) they need to sprint to the halfway line – this time to play defence against 3 and 5. Defenders X1 and X2 will join the back of the queue behind 4 and 5.

Use/purpose: Ability to play defence in a 2 vs 2 situation is being practised (with the ability to help a teammate during the attacker's drive also being developed). Apart from this, a quick reaction from offence to defence is another purpose of the drill.

Materials and equipment required: One ball; a half court with one basket.

Coaching points: Players need to be encouraged to:

- Be active in defence – put pressure on the attacking player right outside the 3 points semicircle by having active feet and active hands, stay low on the feet, with arms wide open – maintain a good defensive position. Do not allow the attacking player to drive through the middle of the court (do not give the middle) – force them sideline–baseline.
- Always talk when playing defence and let their teammate know what is going on (for example 'I've got the ball', 'help').
- For the attacker: protect the ball with non-dribbling hand and with their foot/body.

PROGRESSION:

- Play 2 vs 2 without dribble or with a limited number of dribbles – for example one dribble per player (they can dribble only once each time they have the ball).
- If the attackers score, then the defenders X1 and X2 will stay and play defence once again (this time against attackers 3 and 5) until they (X1 and X2) will get a stop (for example defensive rebound, steal, interception).

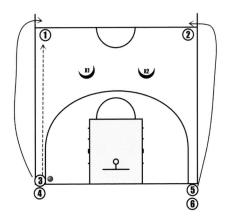

Fig. 142 2 vs 2 continuous drill on half court – initial set-up.

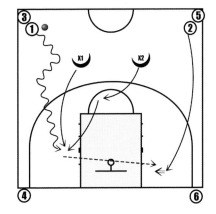

Fig. 143 2 vs 2 continuous drill on half court – with X1 and X2 playing defence.

1 vs 1 GO UNDER THE SCREEN DRILL

Description: In pairs, one player is attacker and the other one is a defender. When the drill starts, they give a 'high five' to each other then player 1 will attack the basket by dribbling sideline–baseline and by going around the cones. Defender X1 will go under the cones (which can be considered a screen) and will play defence in a 1 vs 1 situation (*see* Fig. 144). The drill will finish when the attacker scores (or loses the ball) or when the defender gets a defensive stop (such as a defensive rebound, steal or blocks the shot).

Use/purpose: The drill is used to practise having to go under a screen (the cones that are on the floor) set up by attackers when playing defence. It develops the communication between the teammates when playing defence (when the drill becomes 2 vs 2). It is used at any time during the season when the coach wants to work on defence.

Materials and equipment required: One ball; two cones (or two chairs) that are set up on a half court.

Coaching points: Players need to be encouraged to:
- Be active in defence – make sure they have active feet and active hands (stay low on their feet, with arms wide open – maintain a good defensive position).
- Go under the screen (under the cones/chairs) by running and try to locate the attacker immediately – when they get back into the defensive position (as above).
- Always talk when playing defence and let their teammate know what is going on (for example 'under, under!' or 'help!').

PROGRESSION:
- The coach will limit the time available to player 1 to take a shot – for example will allow six to eight seconds.
- The drill could progress to a 2 vs 2 situation. Attacking player 2 will start on the corner while X2 is their defender. Defender X2 helps on attacker 1's drive then will get back to defend their player (attacker 2 starts on the corner) as seen in Fig. 145.

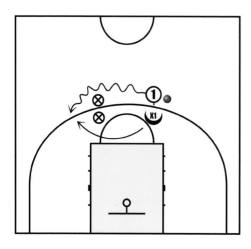

Fig. 144 1 vs 1 go under the screen drill.

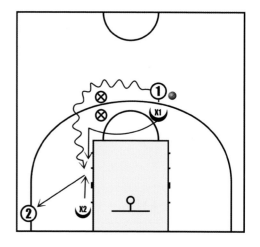

Fig. 145 1 vs 1 go under the screen drill – continuation in a 2 vs 2 scenario.

2 VS 2, 4 VS 2 AND 4 VS 4 FULL COURT DRILL

Description: The drill starts as a 2 vs 2 full court game, with players A1 and A2 attacking against defenders B1 and B2 (see Fig. 146), with players A3, A4, B3 and B4 waiting just outside the court. As soon as the attackers A1 and A2 score or the defenders B1 and B2 get a defensive stop (such as a steal, defensive rebound or intercept the ball), the drill becomes 4 vs 2 with players B3 and B4 joining B1 and B2 in offence against A1 and A2 who now become defenders (see Fig. 147). Once the 4 vs 2 action is over (either the attackers B1, B2, B3 and B4 score or defenders A1 and A2 manage to get a stop), the drill becomes 4 vs 4 – players A3 and

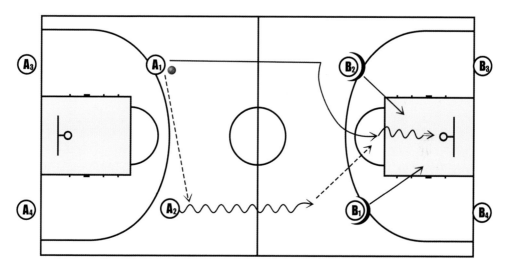

Fig. 146 2 vs 2, 4 vs 2 and 4 vs 4 full court drill – initial 2 vs 2 action.

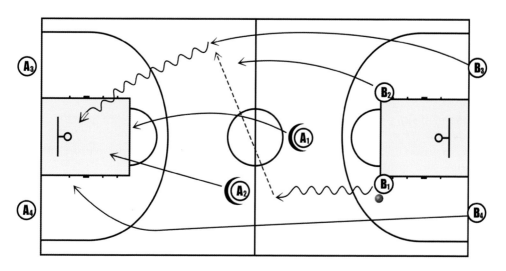

Fig. 147 2 vs 2, 4 vs 2 and 4 vs 4 full court drill – continuation with 4 vs 2 action.

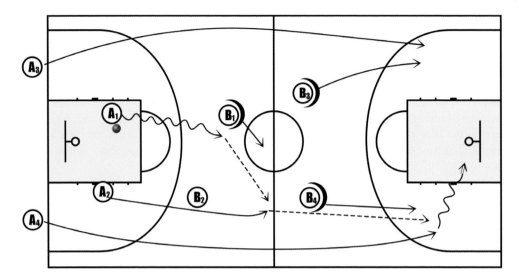

Fig. 148 2 vs 2, 4 vs 2 and 4 vs 4 full court drill – continuation with 4 vs 4 action.

A4 are now joining A1 and A2 who will now play offence against B1, B2, B3 and B4 players (*see* Fig. 148). The coach will allow two actions in 4 vs 4 format and then the drill will restart again following the same pattern (2 vs 2, 4 vs 2, 4 vs 4).

Use/purpose: Players practise playing defence on full court in 2 vs 2 and 4 vs 4 set up and also playing defence when outnumbered by attackers (in 2 against 4 part of the drill). The drill can also be used as a conditioning exercise when players are not allowed to dribble. Additionally, offence is being practised too (as part of the quick offence concept) and also the ability to switch quickly from defence to offence and vice versa. Coaches can implement this drill in their practice at any moment during the season.

Materials and equipment required: One ball; one full court with two baskets.

Coaching points: Players need to be encouraged to:
- For the defenders – have active feet and active hands all the time. Be proactive and meet the ball in order to stop the drive as soon as they can.

- Use fake moves in order to get the ball handler to catch the ball and to force a bad shot and/or a bad pass.
- Talk to each other so that everyone knows who is guarding who.
- For the attackers – play an active part in the team's offence by sprinting forward each time they do not have the ball (get open).
- For the ball carrier – attack and drive to the opposite basket as directly and as quickly as possible.

PROGRESSION:
- The drill can be played up to a specific number of points – first team to score 5 (or 10, 12 and so on).
- The attacking players are not allowed to dribble during the drill (or only during the 4 vs 2 action).
- The number of defensive stops can be counted instead of counting the points that are being scored.

CLOSE OUT FROM BEHIND THE BASELINE WARMING-UP DRILL

Description: Players are grouped in two queues just behind the baseline, under the basket, on both sides of the key. Players 1 and 2 will start the drill at the same time by sprinting forward and closing out on an imaginary shooter who is at the 3 points semicircle (the cone in front of them). After this straight-line sprint move, they will go towards the closest sideline by using defensive slides. Once they touch the sideline, they start a defensive slides backwards move, towards the baseline (*see* Fig. 149) and after this they join the opposite queue so that they have another go on the other side. When players 1 and 2 start their move towards the sideline, players 3 and 4 will start their turn.

Use/purpose: The drill could be used as a warm-up drill and also as a way to learn and practise the close out move (together with the defensive slides move). The ability to sprint and to stop and change direction quickly is also being developed.

Materials and equipment required: One half court with clear markings on; two cones.

Coaching points: Players need to be encouraged to:

- Sprint towards the cone and have at least one arm fully extended high and upwards as if they are trying to block someone's shot, preferably both arms up (*see* Fig. 150).
- The last few steps before they close out (before they reach the cone) are a bit

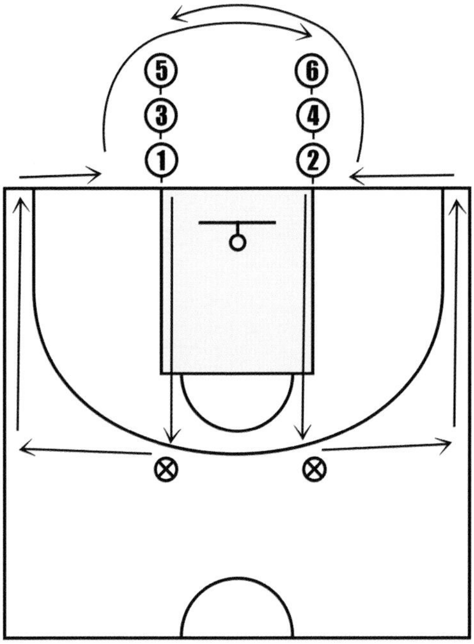

Fig. 149 Close out from behind the baseline warming-up drill.

Fig. 150 Player who is closing out on a shooter with both arms up.

smaller, which will allow them to stop and then be able to change direction quickly.

- Not jump on approaching the cone.
- Stay low during the defensive slides moves and do not cross their legs. Do not jump upwards during the move.
- Talk when approaching the cone, such as 'ball, ball, ball!'.

PROGRESSION:

- Once they arrive in front of the cone spend three to four seconds on the spot with their arms fully extended, as if they are pressuring an attacking player who finished their dribble; afterwards they continue their defensive slides move towards the sideline of the court.

CLOSE OUT ON FULL COURT DRILL

Description: Three players will start the drill at the same time by sprinting forward and closing out with the left hand up at the free throw line level. From here, the same players will continue to run forward and will close out with the right hand up, this time at the halfway line (*see* Fig. 151). The last two close out actions will be at the opposite free throw line with left hand up and then with right hand up again at the end line of the court. Once they are here, the initial three players will wait for the next set of three players, who will have their go following the same pattern and so on.

Use/purpose: This is a great way to practise the close out move and the use of arms when closing out. Sprinting on short distances is being developed and the ability to slow down after running at high speed is also practised and enhanced. The drill can be used as part of the warm up but also in the main part of a session.

Materials and equipment required: One full court with clear markings.

Coaching points: Players need to be encouraged to:

- Sprint forward with big strides and use their arms around their body when running. Fully extend the arm up, as if they would block the shot.
- The last few steps before they close out (before they stop) are a bit smaller, which will allow them to stop quickly.
- Not jump on approaching the spot where they stop.

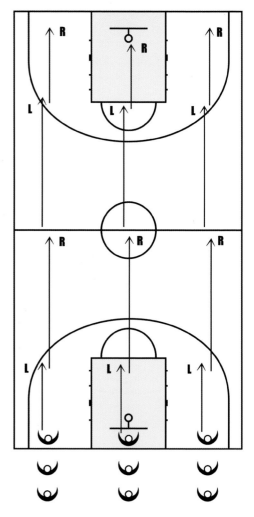

Fig. 151 Close out on full court drill.

- Talk when approaching the spot where they stop, such as 'ball, ball, ball!'.

PROGRESSION:

- Once they arrive at the places where they stop (free throw line, halfway line, the other free throw line, the end line) spend three to four seconds on the spot with the arms fully extended as if pressuring an attacking player who finished their dribble; and afterwards they continue their move towards the next spot.

CLOSE OUT AND DEFENSIVE SLIDES COMBINED WITH LAY-UPS DRILL (HALF COURT AND FULL COURT)

Description: Players are grouped in two queues just behind the baseline, under the basket, on both sides of the key. Players 1 and 2 will start the drill at the same time by sprinting diagonally across the key and closing out on an imaginary shooter who is at the cone at the elbow – player 1 goes to cone B and player 2 goes to cone A. After this straight-line sprint move, they will go towards the closest sideline by using defensive slides: player 1 towards cone D and player 2 towards cone C (*see* Fig. 152). Once they touch the sideline, they start sprinting towards the halfway line and this is when they will start an easy jog move across the court in order to switch queues. When players 1 and 2 start their move towards the sideline (after the close out), players 3 and 4 start their turn.

Use/purpose: The drill could be used as a warm up and also as a way to learn and practise the close out move (together with the defensive slides move). The ability to sprint and to stop and change direction quickly is also being developed.

Materials and equipment required: One full court with clear markings on.

Coaching points: Players need to be encouraged to:

- Sprint towards the cone and close out with both arms fully extended high and upwards as if they are trying to block someone's shot.

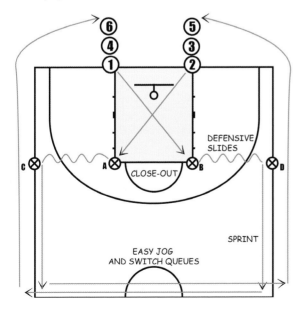

Fig. 152 Close out and defensive slides drill (half court).

133

- The last few steps before they close out (before they reach the cone) are a bit smaller (small stride), which will allow them to stop and then be able to change direction quickly.
- Not jump on approaching the cone.
- Stay low during the defensive slides moves and do not cross their legs. Do not jump upwards during the move.

PROGRESSION:

- The drill can be modified in the following manner: two players at the same time (1 and 5) will perform two consecutive close out moves interspersed with defensive slides back to where they start their turn (right under the basket). Player 1 is closing out to cone A, then back under the basket using defensive slides, then another close out move towards cone B, followed by defensive slides back under the basket; from here 1 will sprint on fastbreak and will receive a pass from passing player P1 in order to go and take a lay-up at the other basket (see Fig. 153). Player 5 will do the same on the opposite side (goes to cone D, then cone C and finally sprint to receive from passing player P2 in order to take a lay-up at the opposite basket).
- Same as in previous drill but this time the move backwards to the place under the basket will be a run backwards move (instead of defensive slides – b and d = run backwards).
- Once players arrive at the cones where they stop, spend three to four seconds on the spot with the arms fully extended as if they would pressure an attacking player

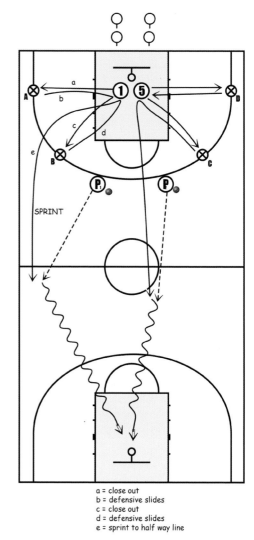

a = close out
b = defensive slides
c = close out
d = defensive slides
e = sprint to half way line

Fig. 153 Close out and defensive slides combined with lay-ups drill (on full court).

who finished their dribble; afterwards they continue the move towards the next spot.

DEFENCE IN A 1 vs 1 SITUATION ON FULL COURT DRILL

Description: In pairs, all players will play 1 vs 1 on a full court one pair at a time (see Fig. 154). The drill starts live (at one end of the court) from the 'go' signal and players will try to score against each other. The normal rules of the game will apply (with regards to travel, double dribble, fouls – offence and defence, five seconds, and so on). If the defender manages to steal the ball, then they will try to score straight away while the offensive player will become an active defender. They play for two minutes and then another pair will do the same.

Use/purpose: The drill is used in order to develop defending ability in a 1 vs 1 situation. Defenders are instructed to apply full court pressure and make it difficult for the attacking player to dribble and attack the basket. Being played on full court, it will also enhance the aerobic capacity of the players (fitness) alongside the ability to dribble the ball under pressure.

Materials and equipment required: One ball between two players; full basketball court, free of any obstructions (no cones or benches).

Coaching points: Players need to be encouraged to:

- Be active as a defender and use both feet to move – try to stay on the imaginary line between the player they are guarding and their own basket.
- Not cross their legs when moving and not to jump.
- Use hands (arms extended) to put additional pressure on the ball.
- For the attacker: always protect the ball and keep their head up when dribbling.

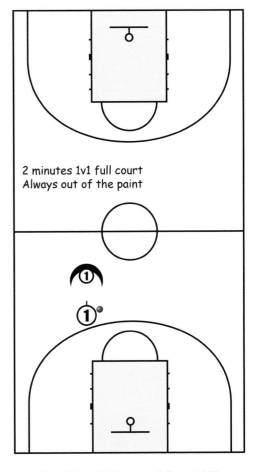

2 minutes 1v1 full court
Always out of the paint

Fig. 154 1 vs 1 defence on full court drill.

PROGRESSION: The drill can be progressed by additional various constraints such as limit the number of dribbles for the offensive player, play continuously for a specified duration (such as thirty seconds; one minute; four minutes), shots can be taken only from outside the key.

DEFENCE IN A 1 vs 1 SITUATION ON A HALF COURT (AFTER GOING AROUND THE CONE MOVE)

Description: In pairs, players are lined up behind the baseline, at either side of the basket. At the starting signal, the player with the ball starts dribbling to the cone that is in front of them (placed at the elbow) and by going round the cone will try to attack the basket in order to score a lay-up. The player without the ball will follow the same pattern (run around the cone) and will try to play defence against the player with the ball as soon as they both go round the cones (*see* Fig. 155).

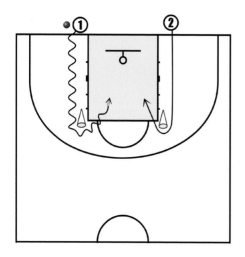

Fig. 155 1 vs 1 defence on half court drill (after going around the cone)

Use/purpose: Playing defence as a half court game during the positional game and not allowing an easy shot to be made. Also, it develops the ability to finish under pressure (pressure of knowing a defender is coming and trying to stop the drive).

Materials and equipment required: One ball between two players; space within the actual basketball hoop.

Coaching points: For the defender – active feet and hands when defending; constant pressure as soon as they meet the attacker after going round the cone. For the attacking player – keep the ball when dribbling away from the defender and protect it; limit the number of dribbles and be as direct to the basket as possible.

PROGRESSION: The focus can be on finishing with a right-hand or left-hand lay-up; finishing with a jump shot; finishing within a set time limit (three to four seconds); finishing after a set number of dribbles (two to three maximum). The defender needs to attempt to block the shot or focus on stealing the ball from the dribble.

FINISH UNDER PRESSURE IN 1 vs 1 SITUATION ON HALF COURT DRILL

Description: Players are working in pairs with one ball between two. Player 1 is the attacker (they have the ball) while player 2 is a defender and they start side by side (*see* Fig. 156). At the starting signal (such as a whistle or clap), they will sprint at the same time towards the middle of court, go round the cone in front of them and then they will play 1 vs 1 – player 1 will dribble, trying to score a lay-up preferably while player 2 will play defence trying to stop 1 from scoring. As soon as player 1 goes round the cone they will immediately attack the basket without waiting for player 2 to come and play defence. If player 1 misses the first shot, they can get the offensive rebound and try to score again. The drill will finish when the defender gets a defensive stop (such as a steal, defensive rebound or blocks the shot) or when the attacker scores. Players will then change roles and the drill continues.

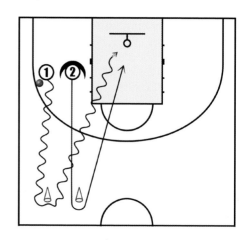

Fig. 156 Finish under pressure in 1 vs 1 situation on half court drill.

Use/purpose: While the intention is to work on defence (such as sprint trying to stop the attacker, trying to block the shot, rebounding), another purpose of the drill is to play offence – ability to dribble and score under the pressure of a defender is being worked on. Use this drill in the main part of a session after players have had a good warm up.

Materials and equipment required: One ball between two players; two cones and one half of a basketball court.

Coaching points: Players need to be encouraged to:

- Keep their head up when dribbling the ball.
- Protect the ball when the defender is active (for example if/when the defender

is on their right side, this is when they need to dribble with the left hand and vice versa).

- For defenders, try to put pressure on the attacker as soon as the defender goes round the cone – active hands and active feet in order to force a shot as far away as possible from the basket; try to contest the shot; box out and do not give the attacker a second chance.

PROGRESSION:

- The attacker will have four dribbles maximum (or three only with more advanced players) after going around the cone.
- The attacker will need to take a jump shot instead of a lay-up.

BOX OUT IN PAIRS DRILL

Description: One ball between two players – player 1 has the ball (offence) while player 2 is in defence. They are at about 3–4m away from each other (*see* Fig. 157). Player 2 (the defender) starts the drill by running towards

the attacker, makes contact with their forearm, rolls in front of the attacker and then will box out. During the defender's initial approach move, player 1 will throw the ball gently upwards so that it lands just in front of them;

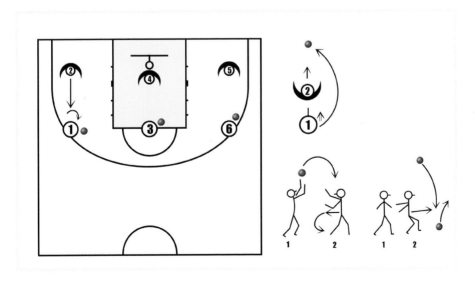

Fig. 157 Box out in pairs drill.

this is when the defender will step forward to collect the ball that will bounce off the floor.

Use/purpose: The drill is intended to get the defender to learn and apply the steps that are needed when boxing out defensively: approach the shooter, make contact with the forearm, roll and box out, then step forward to get/to rebound the ball.

Materials and equipment required: One ball between two players; one area of the court free of any obstructions.

Coaching points: Players need to be encouraged to:

- Make contact with the defender using their forearm – look at the shooter initially

and then look at the ball (box out first and then go for the ball).

- Roll and box out while staying low, with knees flexed, so that the attacker cannot push them easily and a jumping action can be performed immediately.
- Fully extend arms when going to get the ball.

PROGRESSION:

- Use a pivoting move as soon as they secure the ball in order to protect it from the attacker, who now becomes defender.

SHOOTING, BOXING OUT AND REBOUNDING DRILL IN PAIRS

Description: Six players are grouped in pairs as in Fig. 158, with players 1, 2 and 3 having a ball each while A, B and C are defenders. One pair at a time – player 1 takes a shot and this is when defender A will box out and then both must go and get the rebound. Once one of them has got the ball and they finish the action, the next pair will have their go and so on. Five possessions for each player and then players change roles, A, B and C will become attackers while 1, 2 and 3 will be defenders.

Use/purpose: This drill gets the players to learn, practise and refine the boxing out action and going for the rebound as a consequence of guarding the ball (after a shot is made).

Materials and equipment required: One ball between two players; one basket on one half court.

Coaching points: Players need to be encouraged to:

- Approach/locate the attacker, box out first and then look to go and get the ball.
- Try to be on their toes instead of being flat footed at the beginning of the action so that they can move quickly into a box out position.

- Assume all the shots are missed and go and get the rebound.

PROGRESSION:

- If the attacker gets the offensive rebound then both players play 'live' 1 vs 1 at that basket.

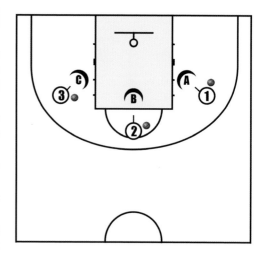

Fig. 158 Shooting, boxing out and rebounding drill in pairs.

4 VS 4 BOX OUT DRILL

Description: Two teams of four players are positioned as in Fig. 159: four defenders are lined up right in front of the basket in the middle of the key and four attacking players on the 3 points semicircle. The coach (or passing player) has the ball and will start the drill by passing the ball to any of the four attackers (for example pass to player 1) and at the same time will also call a number between one and four. If they say 'four' for example, defender X4 will sprint to where the ball was passed (sprint to 1) and will close out without jumping. Player 1 will take the shot and everyone else (X1, X2 and X3) will need to match up and box out all the remaining three attackers who are on the perimeter (2, 3 and 4). The drill can be played until a team scores five times – if the defensive team gets the rebound (without attackers scoring) then they will switch roles and become attackers.

Use/purpose: The drill develops the ability of a defender to locate an opposite player and box them out. Reaction to the signal coming from the coach (the number called) is being developed too alongside the ability to box out and to rebound (both offensive rebounding and defensive rebounding).

Materials and equipment required: One ball; eight to ten players and one half court.

Coaching points: Players need to be encouraged to:
- Pay full attention to the number called by the coach.
- Sprint to close out the shot, initiate contact with the forearm, box out and then go and get the rebound.
- If the ball is in the air – jump to get the rebound; do not wait for the ball to come to them.

PROGRESSION:
- Player 1 will pass to 2 (or to another player) and 2 will shoot.
- Player 1 can dribble once and take the shot.
- Once the rebound is secured by the defending team, all players can now play live towards the other basket and then back.

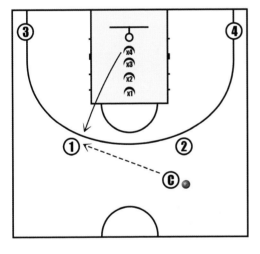

Fig. 159 4 vs 4 box out drill.

DEFENCE AND DEFENSIVE SLIDES AND MOVES DRILL

Description: All players are spaced out (about 2–3m between them) on one side of the court as shown in Fig. 160. They start by adopting a low stance, well-balanced defensive position, with feet wide apart on the spot they occupy – similar to the stance adopted by the player in Fig. 161. At the coach's signal, all players will start moving from the sideline towards the middle of the court using defensive slides in the following manner: using very small steps (while going sideways), they need to maintain the defensive position all the way from the sideline up to the imaginary line that divides the court into two equal parts (the dotted line

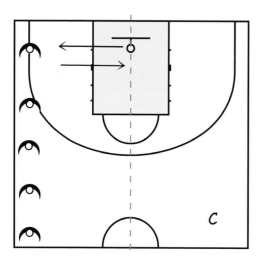

Fig. 160 Defence and defensive slides and moves drill.

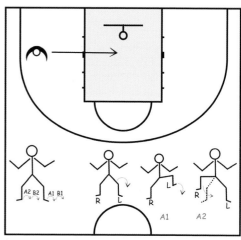

Fig. 162 Defence and defensive slides and moves drill – steps sequence.

Fig. 161 Player in a very low stance/player in a defending position.

in Fig. 160). The first two to three goes (sideline to middle of court and back equals one go) will be performed very slowly, with a focus on maintaining the low position, with arms wide open (out), back straight, feet pointing slightly outwards. The next two to three goes will still be slow but this time each player will take one side step (left foot followed by right foot) using the count of 'one–two' and then stop (pause, stay still on the spot) for a moment according to the following sequence: steps A1+A2 then stop for one to two seconds and then steps B1+B2 and so on – everything at very slow speed (see Fig. 162). These repetitions will be followed by the next two to three goes (or more), which will be performed with an increase in speed.

Use/purpose: The drill is used in order to teach the fundamental position in defence and also the side movement using defensive slides. It is very useful and efficient with beginners but also even with more advanced players who constantly need to practise the fundamental defensive moves. It can be used in any part of the season and also in any part of the training session.

Materials and equipment required: One half court; some court markers or cones could be used too.

Coaching points: Players need to be encouraged to:

- Maintain a very low body position, with knees flexed/bent and arms wide open.
- Keep the back straight, without learning forward or sideways.
- Not jump at any time during the slides – try to stay on the floor all the time.
- Keep their head up and arms wide out at all times.

PROGRESSION:

- When it's their go, players should take two small steps followed by one longer step while still going sideways. So the sequence will be A1A2 – B1B2 (all these with small steps) followed immediately by C1C2 long step (see Fig. 163) and so on.
- Increase the distance that is covered by the defenders from sideline to the other sideline.
- Combine and alternate the sideways move(s) with running forwards and/or backwards.
- Work in pairs – ask one of the players to mirror the moves of the other one, who will be the defender, and choose what kind of steps to take (such as small, big, two or three consecutive).

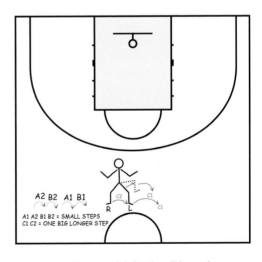

Fig. 163 Defence and defensive slides and moves drill – steps sequence (continuation).

4 VS 3 +1 TRANSITION DEFENCE DRILL

Description: All players are divided into two groups of four: players 1, 2, 3 and 4 are attackers (and they start on the baseline under basket A) while players X1, X2, X3 and X4 are defenders (and they are situated level with the free throws line at the same basket). Passing player P (who can be a coach) has the ball and they will pass to any of the attackers. The rule of the drill is this: the defensive player who is in front of the attacker who receives the ball from P will need to sprint to touch the baseline (when their corresponding attacker receives the ball – without obstructing the dribbler) and then to sprint back in defence while the four attackers will play 4 vs 3 towards basket B against the remaining three defenders. So, for example, player 3 receives the ball – as illustrated in Fig.164 – and this is when defender X3 will sprint to touch the baseline; at the same time, players 1, 2, 3 and 4 will attack towards basket B and will try to use the numerical advantage that they have temporarily. They will look to play quickly and to score against X1, X2 and X4 early during the possession until X3 arrives. If the attackers do not manage to score, the drill will become 4 vs 4 as X3 will sprint back to join their teammates and their defensive efforts. The drill will continue whether attackers score or not in the following way: if 1, 2, 3 or 4 score, then X1, X2, or X4 (or even X3 when they arrive) will come inbound from behind basket B and will now become attackers trying to score at basket A against the other 4 players who will now need to defend. If 1, 2, 3 or 4 do not score or when X1, X2, X3 or X4 get a defensive stop (such as an interception, steal, force a turnover, or a defensive rebound) then they will get the ball and play 4 vs 4 straight away towards basket A. After this 4 vs 4 game, players will re-start the drill by switching roles (switch offence with defence).

Use/purpose: It is a very useful drill to learn defensive transition when being outnumbered (and at the same time to learn how to attack the basket when having an extra player and a temporary advantage). Quick thinking and quick decision-making (what do I do with the ball, who do I pass it to, who do I guard?) are required from all players and are developed (irrespective of role; defender or attacking player). The drill can be used in the main part of the session and it is also very good for pre-season training.

Materials and equipment required: One ball; one full court with two baskets.

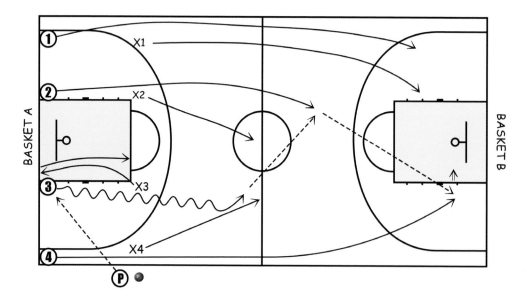

Fig. 164 4 vs 3 +1 transition defence drill – initial starting set-up.

Coaching points: Players need to be encouraged to:
- For defenders:
  - o The two defenders who are the closest to the player who receives the ball (X2 and X4 in Fig. 164) will try to stop the drive to the basket and force a pass (do not allow a coast-to-coast lay-up).
  - o Make sure they sprint back in defence and try to be on the same level with the wing players who will look to sprint on fastbreak in order to receive and score easy points.
  - o Defenders X1, X2 and X4's main objective is to slow attackers down so that X3 comes back in defence and the group plays 4 vs 4 instead of 3 vs 4.
- For attackers:
  - o Try to sprint on fastbreak if they do not have the ball in order to receive the pass and score.
  - o If they receive the ball, try to initiate the fastbreak (and the quick offence) by dribbling in a straight line towards the basket where they score. Always keep the head up when dribbling in order to see any of their teammates who are in a better position, so that they can pass the ball to them.

PROGRESSION:
- With more experienced/advanced teams, the coach can ask the players to play without dribbling the ball (so it will be just be pass and shoot without dribble).
- The coach will indicate a number ('X1') and that defender will sprint to touch the baseline irrespective of where the pass from P goes to. So for example the coach will shout 'X1' and the pass goes to attacker 4 – this is when X1 will sprint to touch the baseline and not X4. From here the drill continues as described previously.

Conclusion

The role of the coach is 'to manage the process', according to Cross and Lyle when they talk about coaching as a process (2002, page 8) – a gradual, time-consuming process that should benefit from detailed planning amongst other elements and resources. Planning as a skill is a vital component in a coach's repertoire. As a consequence, coaches need to be clear when they decide what to include in their planning documents when it comes to their delivery of basketball, and this can be performed as part of training (or session) plans. For example, what exercises and drills do I use? How many reps? How long for? Full court or half court? How – individually or in pairs or with the whole team? When during the season? In this context, session plans are useful tools that will help coaches implement their philosophy in practice. Appendices 1 to 5 contain samples of such session plans that are provided as examples from practice – some of these plans are very brief and simplistic in their content (*see* Appendices 1 and 2) while other ones are very detailed (*see* session plans in Appendices 3, 4 and 5). As in any other area of life, some people give more attention to things than others; the same applies to the world of coaching: there are coaches who are very detailed when it comes to planning (which we

strongly encourage) while there are also others who think it will be enough to have just a few points written on the paper. There is no unique template that could be used by all coaches and some coaches might actually prefer to start with a blank piece of paper – nothing wrong with this approach! However, having a plan when going into a coaching session is a must. In general, it is better to over-plan or plan more than you need, such as plan more drills and activities for the session, rather than under-plan – it is difficult to go in front of the team and try to invent something on the spot, especially for the young coaches who might have limited experience. The amount of planning will impact directly on the quality of the training that you provide and consequently, in the medium and long term, on the quality of the players and teams that you will produce.

The old Latin saying *'Repetitio est mater studiorum'* translates as 'repetition is the mother of all learning' or 'practice makes perfect'. The game has grown, transformed and developed in recent years, partly due to the impact that some great players and coaches have had on its overall development, combined with some rule changes designed to make the game even more appealing and dynamic. Despite these facts, some principles, ideas, drills and concepts that were 'modern' some time ago are still applicable even nowadays. One aspect that will constantly be present in the sports coaching world is the need to work hard in order to get better. On top of this is the continuous desire to try to learn the game and be aware of all the trends or ideas that will inevitably appear. Having a curious mind will allow you to do this – to learn, especially from more experienced and successful coaches; countries such as Lithuania, Spain, Serbia and France regularly produce good-quality coaches and good players (and teams) and there are lots of things to learn from them. By being open, by creating and maintaining communication channels with players and the people around the game (such as other coaches, parents and supporters) your chances of succeeding as a coach will increase. 'Having fun' should be something constantly in your mind as a coach and part of your approach to training and games!

BIBLIOGRAPHY

Bauer, R. (2018) 'Transition defence – concepts and drills'. Presentation delivered at the Coaching Clinic for junior coaches delivered for Romanian Basketball Federation in Oradea (Romania) – personal notes.

Beeching, K. (2011) 'Planning and periodisation'. In Navin, A. (Ed.) *Sports Coaching for Students, Coaches and Competitors*, UK: Crowood Press.

Cross, N. (2002) Chapter 9. 'Individualization of training programmes' (pp 174–191), cited in Cross, N. and Lyle, J. (2002) *The Coaching Process – Principles and Practice for Sport.* Butterworth-Heinemann: Oxford.

Cross, N. and Lyle, J. (2002) *The Coaching Process – Principles and Practice for Sport.* Butterworth-Heinemann: Oxford.

Douge, B. and Hastie, P. (1993) 'Coaching effectiveness'. *Sport Science Review*, 2 (2), pp 14–29.

Kemzura, K. (2015) 'Individual development of perimeter players'. Presentation delivered at the International Coaching Clinic for Basketball Coaches in Kaunas (Lithuania) – personal notes.

Kemzura, K. (2022) 'Inside and perimeter players' skill development', online at FIBA Europe Coaching Website Coaches' Section, available at: https://coaching.fibaeurope.com/default.asp?cid=%7B87FFFFCD-C6BB-4BBD-8975-4B26F438B4BE%7D (accessed on 20th March 2022)

Meurs, P. (2018) 'Individual and team defence concepts'. Presentation delivered at the Belgian Basketball Coaching Clinic Event 2018 in Duffel (Belgium) – personal notes.

Pike, F. (2001) *Better Coaching: Advanced Coach's Manual* (2nd edition). Australian Sports Commission: Human Kinetics.

Radu, A. (2015) *Basketball Coaching: Putting Theory into Practice.* London: Bloomsbury.

Sports Coach UK (2007) *Planning and Periodisation.* Coachwise Business Solutions.

APPENDICES

APPENDIX 1

EXAMPLE OF A PRACTICE PLAN DURING THE SEASON (90 MINUTES SESSION; 6.00–7.30 PM)

Team: .... Location: .... Date and time: ....

Number of players: .... Aims: ....

Timing	Length/ duration	Activity	Proposed drills/content
6.00–6.02	2 min	Intro/aims/ updates	• Announce aims. • Briefly review previous game result.
6.02–6.12	10 min	Warm up	• Coast-to-coast shooting. • Stretching (dynamic).
6.12–6.32	20 min	Offensive drills	• Practise offensive sets vs man-to-man defence. • Work on half court and full court. • Semiactive and active defenders.
6.32–6.52	20 min	Work for defence	• 1 vs 1 and 2 vs 2 on half court. • Box out and rebounding.
6.52–7.27	35 min	Full court game	• 5 vs 5 with substitutions. • Full court scrimmage.
7.27–7.30	3 min	Cool down	• Form shooting. • In pairs – 5 shots each then rotate (x3)

Appendix 2

Example of a Practice Plan During Pre-season (Ninety Minutes Session; Indoor)

Date:	Monday 14 March 2022		Staff/ Coach(es)	(initials of coaches delivering the session)
Theme/ Aim(s):	*Session aims and objectives:* Shooting practice (shooting in pairs and as a team) Pre-season/~~season~~/~~post season~~ (circle)		Session number and location:	*Session no:* On-court/~~video room~~/ ~~S&C room~~ (circle/specify)
Time	**Organization of activity/Drills**	**Coach to lead activity**	**Key coaching points** (use them when teaching/coaching)	
19:00	Warm up	S&C	As per the instructions provided by the S&C coach.	
19:10	Shooting while running drills • full court – pull up shots **Drill:** Shooting drill in three players with two balls (full court) (see full details, coaching points and progression inside the book)	all	Follow through. Be well balanced.	
19:20	Shooting in pairs • on half court **Drill:** Shooting in pairs (with own rebounding) drill (see full details, coaching points and progression inside the book)	all	Have arms out ready to catch. Same as above.	
19:40	Water break	all	NA	
19:42	Free throws • sets of 5 throws x 3 • in pairs (one shooting and one rebounding)	all	Elbow under the ball; follow through; Focus and concentration.	
19:50	Shooting from offensive sets • plays vs man-to-man defence • plays vs zone	all	Timing of actions (screens, cuts, passes). Pass the ball on time.	
20:10	Shooting competition • two teams/one team at each basket. • play '33' • shoot from the top of key	all	Shout the score with loud voice. Focus on your own shot – leave arm extended after each shot; follow through.	
20:20	Cool down	S&C	As per the instructions provided by the S&C coach.	
20:25	Closing remarks/arrangements for next training session 20:30 end of session		NA	

EXAMPLE OF A PRACTICE PLAN – INDIVIDUALIZATION FOR CENTRES (SIXTY MINUTES)

Individualization U18 boys – centres

DATE	TIME	VENUE	NUMBER OF PLAYERS	EQUIPMENT/RESOURCES
	7.00–8.00pm	Sports hall at…	Expected: 6 players Present:	6 basketballs 6 chairs

SESSION AIMS:

- To improve shooting and play facing the basket and with back to the basket.
- To work on/continue improving rebounding ability.

NOTE: Two centres from U16 team will join this session.

INTRO/WARM UP & Stretching

2 min 10 lengths easy jog while dribbling – full court;
– right-hand dribble on the way to the opposite basket and left-hand dribble on the way back.
8–10 min Warm up – stretching upper body (incl. shoulders, elbows, wrists)
– stretching lower body (knees, ankles, hips).
5–6 min Warm-up shooting drill – drill *Elbow and short corner shooting for centres* (*see* book).
Score 15 as a whole group.
1 min water break

MAIN PART

8–10 min Drill; *Elbow shooting for centres* (*see* book).
Corrections/focus on: correct shooting mechanic; footwork; follow through; have arms ready to receive.
10–12 min Drill: *Short corner shooting.*
Add defender and make it 1 vs 1 drill.
5 min Free throws shooting – in pairs/sets of 5 FTs and rotate.
1 min water break
8–10 min Rebounding:
Drill *Throw the ball onto the backboard above the ring and get the rebound.*
Add defender after 5 reps per player.

CLOSING/Warm down

4–5 min. Free throws shooting – sets of 2 FTs x 3 sets/in pairs.

Closing remarks/notes

- provide individual advice to players with regards to what they still need to work on.

APPENDIX 4

EXAMPLE OF A PRACTICE PLAN

JUNIOR TEAM U14 boys

DATE	TIME	VENUE	NUMBER OF PLAYERS	EQUIPMENT
Friday 12 November 2021	6.30–8.00 pm	Sports hall at…	Expected: 12 Present:	• Players bring own ball. • 4 chairs. • 6 cones • 2 sets of bibs (different colours)

SESSION AIMS:

- Fastbreak – to practise 2 vs 1; 3 vs 0 and 3 vs 1 situations. Apply these situations in 5 vs 5 full court game.

Personal coaching goals/NOTES:

- Integrate all abilities into the session/game.

NOTE: Two players are missing because of away trips with school.

INTRO/WARM UP & STRETCHING

- Warm up shooting drill: *spacing game between guard and guard (dribble and pass to the cutting player) (see book)*. Coaching points: 6–8 minutes
- Send a powerful pass to your teammate.
- Synchronize your moves – do not cut to the basket too early before or too late after the dribbling action started.
- Have your hands ready to receive the pass so that you can catch and shoot.
- Stretching – coach led.   8–10 minutes

MAIN PART

2 vs 1 full court; in pairs/one ball between two.
When in defence: one player is playing defence on the free throw line and teammate is waiting on free throw line extended.   4–5 minutes

1' water break
3 vs 0 *Passing in 3s on full court drill (see book)*   6–8 minutes

Coaching points:

- Send good, powerful, accurate passes so that the receiving player runs into the path of the pass.

150

- Keep running forward if you do not have the ball.
- Always catch the ball with both hands.

3 vs 0 *Fastbreak initiated with pass from the corner drill (see book)*   6–8 minutes

3 vs 1 full court;
When in defence – one player from the group of 3 is on FT line while the other two are on FT extended
Play without dribble   4 minutes
Play normal game (dribble allowed)   5–6 minutes
1' water break
5 vs 5 full court game   30–35 minutes
- Play games to 5 points (with 1 and 2 points instead of 2s and 3s).
- Special rule – if you score as a consequence of a fastbreak (from 2 vs 1 and 3 vs 1 situations) = 2 points and possession from halfway line.

CLOSING/Warm down
- One lap around the court with dribble – easy jog.
- Light stretching – players to lead.   3–4 minutes

Closing remarks/notes   1 minute

APPENDIX 5

Detailed Session plan (2 hours training session)

SESSION PLAN

TEAM	COMPETITION Division / League		SEASON 2021 - 2022

DATE	TIME	VENUE	NUMBER OF PLAYERS	EQUIPMENT
Wednesday 1 September 2021	7.00 – 9.00 pm	main sports hall	Expected: 12 Present:	• 12 basketballs • 2 sets of bibs (different colours) • 1 coaching clipboard • Whistle and stopwatch
	DURATION 120'			

SESSION AIMS/GOALS
- To meet the players and find out about their level.
- Light session to incorporate: 1. Ball handling drills; 2. fastbreak drills; 3. Shooting (jump shots and free throws).

PERSONAL COACHING GOALS
- Good time management (start on time; finish on time);
- Control the group firmly but in a fun/enjoyable atmosphere that players can enjoy.

PART	TIME	TASK and GROUP MANAGEMENT	DIAGRAM and COACHING POINTS

Introduction	4 min.
	5 min
	10 min
	6 min.
		• Introductions & session aims/objectives.
		• GAME – "Fish and the net".
		• STATIC STRETCHING – whole team, Assist Coach to lead stretching.
		• DYNAMIC STRETCHING – 6 exercises, full court; on the way back defensive play: ankles moves, knees up, heels up, skipping, long strides run, lift knee up and kick.
		  – 1 set.
		  – 25 sec break between sets - DIAGRAM 1.
			
			Diagram 1

WARM UP (general)			
	3 min.	• **Coast to coast shooting** – individually, jump shots from close distance – first player to score 10 (each basket = 1 point).	Diagram 2

SPECIFIC WARM UP	4 min.	• **Ball handling drills** – one player with 2 balls (jog across the court):
		  – Dribbling 2 balls in the same time.
		  – Dribbling 2 balls alternatively.
		  – Roll one ball and dribble the other one.
		  – Dribble one ball while throwing the other one in the air.
		  See DIAGRAM 2.
			
			– Keep head up.
			– Push the ball hard on the floor.
			Diagram 3.

	5 min.	• **Dribbling and changing direction** – individually (1 ball per player):
		  – change direction & dribble In front of legs (cross over).
		  – Between legs.
		  – Behind the back.
		  – 360° turn (spin move dribble).
		  2-3 minutes for right hand; same for left hand. See DIAGRAM 3	

	10 min.	• **1 vs 1 relationship** in pairs (Attacker vs. Defender). See DIAGRAM 4	

153

PART	TIME	TASK and GROUP MANAGEMENT	DIAGRAM and COACHING POINTS

MAIN PART
 	
SKILL DEVELOPMENT & PRACTICES
	10 min.
	
	5 min.
	
	15 min.
	
	7-8 min.
		• **3 man weave** – groups of 3 players with one ball.
		  – 3 lengths for each group x 5 sets.
		  – 3 passes only allowed.
		  – miss 1 – do one more length. See DIAGRAM 5
		
		• FREE THROWS – in pairs; one ball per pair.
		  – Shoot 4 sets of 5 FT each = 20 in total (count how many you score).
		
		• **Fastbreak 3 vs 2** all the time (ex. in 11 players) – see DIAGRAM 6.
		  – the defender who gets the rebound or intercepts the ball will go 3 vs 2 towards the other end of court with the 2 players waiting at a 45° angle (free throw line extended).
		  – 5 min. normal game;
		  – 5 min. one dribble only.
		  – 5 min. no dribble.
		
		• JUMP SHOTS – 2 teams
		Option A (if 10 players) – 2 teams of 5 players. 5 players with 3 balls shooting drill – see DIAGRAM 7.
		
		Option B (if 11 players or more): 2 teams, 2 balls per team. 5 positions, score 10 as a team and then move to next spot. Aim: to score 30 in total as a team. See DIAGRAM 8.
		
		• FREE THROWS – in pairs; one ball per pair.
		  – Shoot 4 sets of 5 FT each = 20 in total (count how many you score).
			Diagram 4
			
			Diagram 5
			
			Diagram 6

PART	TIME	TASK and GROUP MANAGEMENT	DIAGRAM and COACHING POINTS
	15 min.	• 5 vs 5 FULL COURT GAME – normal game, 1st team to 11. Scoring system: 1 and 2 points. 4 points for a fastbreak.	Diagram 7 Diagram 8
COOL DOWN Wrap up	5 min. 2 min. 3 min.	• FREE THROWS competition – same 2 teams; first team to score 10 = best out of 3 games. Punishment for losing team. • 4 lengths – light jogging. • Final remarks – conclusions.	

COMMENTS/REMARKS

BRIEF ANALYSIS and EVALUATION OF SESSION

Appendix 6

Usual terminology and frequently used terms that were used as part of the book

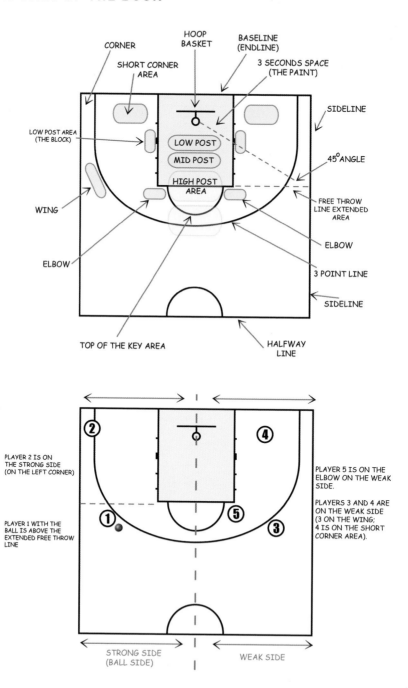

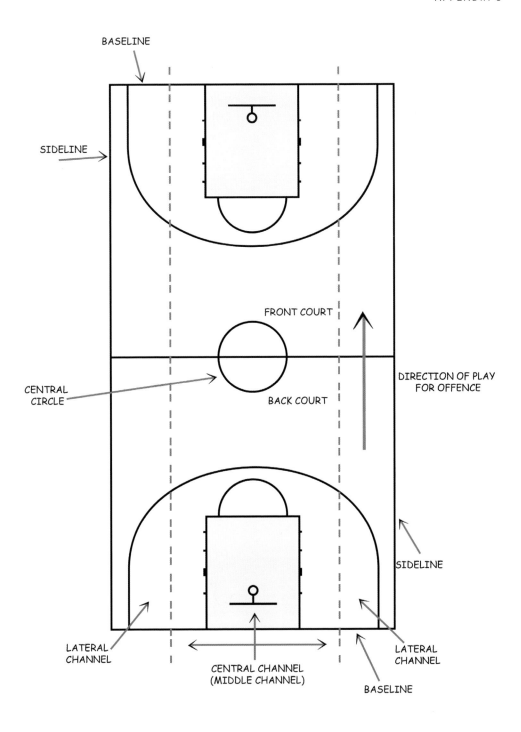

BASELINE

SIDELINE

CENTRAL
CIRCLE

FRONT COURT

BACK COURT

DIRECTION OF PLAY
FOR OFFENCE

SIDELINE

LATERAL
CHANNEL

CENTRAL CHANNEL
(MIDDLE CHANNEL)

LATERAL
CHANNEL

BASELINE

About the authors

Alexandru Radu is currently Senior Lecturer in Sports Coaching Basketball (and Course Leader for the Sport Business Management undergraduate programme) at University of Worcester in the UK. Amongst other lecturing roles, he used to be the Course Leader for the Masters Degree MSc in European Basketball Coaching Science, the programme he delivered at University of Worcester in partnership with Lithuanian Sport University in Kaunas – Lithuania, and also worked at Northumbria University and Gateshead College Sports Academy (both in Newcastle upon Tyne in the UK) and at Al. I. Cuza University of Iasi (in Iasi – Romania). As a basketball coach he coached a wide range of teams and players at both club and national team level including: Assistant Coach of Romania Women's National Team (and participation at the EuroBasket Women 2015), Romania U20 and U18 Women's National Team (and coached at FIBA U20 and U18 European Championship Division B in 2018 and 2019); Assistant Coach of Wales Men National Team (and participation at FIBA European Championship Division C in 2016 Chisinau – Moldova); Head Coach of Wales U18 Men's National Team; Assistant Coach of Worcester Wolves in British Basketball League (BBL); Associate Head Coach of Cardiff Archers Women's British Basketball League (WBBL). Apart from coaching, he also delivered presentations at national and international coaching clinics and camps such as: Belgian Basketball Coaching Clinic Event 2018 in Duffel (Belgium); Edukacine Krepsinio Stovykla (Educational Basketball Camp) in 2014 in Alytus (Lithuania); translator at International Basketball Coaching Clinic Klaipeda in 2011 (organized by Lithuanian Coaches Association) in Klaipeda (Lithuania); key speaker at Basketball Coaching Clinic for the North East region in 2011 in Middlesbrough (England). Some of his previous publications include (selected titles): *The Science of Basketball* (published by Routledge: London, UK in 2018); *Basketball Coaching. Putting Theory into Practice* (published by Bloomsbury: London, UK in 2015) and *Basketball: A Guide to Skills, Techniques and Tactics* (published by Crowood Press: Marlborough, UK in 2010).

Florin Nini is currently Lecturer at Danubius University in Galati (Romania). Before this role he spent twenty-two years at Dunarea de Jos University of Galati in the same city. Alongside lecturing, he held numerous coaching roles including; Head Coach of CSM Galati – senior men's team in Romanian First League (Professional League in Romania); Head Coach of Romanian Women's National Team (and participation at Eurobasket 2015); Head Coach of Romania U18 Men's National Team (and participation at various FIBA European Championships); Head Coach of professional men's teams including: BC Steaua Turabo Bucuresti (Romanian First League); Energia Rovinari Tirgu Jiu (Romanian First League); Pitesti (Romanian First League); Galati (Romanian First League); and CSM Tirgoviste women's team (and participation in Women's Euroleague). Apart from coaching senior teams, he has over twenty years' experience of coaching at youth basketball level. He is the camp director at Phoenix Basketball Camp – a basketball camp for young players that takes place every summer in Galati (Romania). He is the Head of the Commission for the Development of Basketball Coaches as part of the Romanian Basketball Federation and is currently the Assistant Coach of Romanian Men's National Team and Head Coach of Romania U20 Men.

INDEX